JONAH: GRACE FOR SINNERS AND SAINTS

Iain M. Duguid

Study Guide with Leader's Notes

New Growth Press
WWW.NEWGROWTHPRESS.COM

New Growth Press, Greensboro, NC 27401
newgrowthpress.com
Copyright © 2019 by Iain M. Duguid

Cover Design: Faceout Books, faceoutstudio.com
Interior Design and Typesetting: Professional Publishing Services, christycallahan.com
Exercises and Application Questions: Jack Klumpenhower

ISBN: 978-1-948130-65-3 (print)
ISBN: 978-1-948130-66-0 (ebook)

Printed in the United States of America

28 27 23 25 24 23 22 21   3 4 5 6 7

CONTENTS

ABOUT THIS STUDY

Like the other small group resources in this series, *Jonah: Grace for Sinners and Saints* has a distinct focus: Your goal will be bigger than merely to study the book of Jonah. You will also keep your eyes on Jesus and the good news of God's love and power to save you as well as learn how that power takes you beyond yourself to love others—especially those who don't yet know Jesus.

Growing as a Christian is not simply a matter of learning about the Bible or trying hard to live according to it. Instead you must grow in your awareness that you need Jesus every day to help you turn from yourself and turn toward him and others. The heart of the gospel message is to know we need forgiveness, to ask God for forgiveness for Jesus's sake, and then to extend to others the grace we have been given. The message of grace and hope that brought you to Jesus is the same message of the gospel you need to hear every day as you follow Jesus. And it's the same message we get to share with other needy people. *Jonah: Grace for Sinners and Saints* is designed to help you do this in a group. Studying with others will let you benefit from what God is also teaching them, and it will give you encouragement as you apply what you learn.

The group will be a place to share not only successes but also sins and weaknesses, so expect differences in how people participate. It's okay if some in the group are cheery while others are weary, if some "get it" quickly while others want to look more deeply, or if some are eager to share while others take it slowly. But because you'll be studying the Bible and praying together, also expect God's Spirit to work and change people—starting with you!

Each participant should have one of these study guides to join in reading and be able to work through the exercises during that part of the study. The facilitator for each lesson should read through both the lesson and the leader's notes in the back of this book before the lesson begins, but otherwise no preparation or homework is required.

Each lesson will take about an hour to complete, perhaps a bit more if your group is large, and will include these elements:

BIG IDEA. This is a summary of the main point of the lesson.

BIBLE CONVERSATION. You will read a passage or passages from the Bible and discuss what you read. As the heading suggests, the Bible conversation questions are intended to spark a conversation rather than generate correct answers. In most cases, the questions will have several possible good answers and a few best answers.

ARTICLE. This is the main teaching section of the lesson, written by the book's author.

DISCUSSION. The discussion questions following the article will help you apply the teaching to your life. Again, there will be several good ways to answer each question.

EXERCISE. The exercise will be a section of the lesson you complete on your own. You can write in the book if that helps you, or just think about your responses. You will then share some of what you learned with the group. If the group is large, it may help to split up to share the results of the exercise and pray so everyone has a better opportunity to participate.

WRAP-UP AND PRAYER. Prayer is a critical part of the lesson because your spiritual growth will happen through God's work in you, not by your self-effort. You will be asking him to do that good work.

As a character, Jonah is refreshingly honest. You will likely find him saying what you sometimes think but might hesitate to say aloud. As a book, Jonah is full of gospel encouragement. You will see God's compassion for sinners and hear of his long-planned rescue through the death and resurrection of Jesus. And you will feel God's tug on your heart, which calls all who believe to come nearer still to their good, good Father.

1

NOT JUST A
FISH STORY

BIG IDEA

Is Jonah's story yours as well? At first sight, this book about a prophet, a fish, and a hostile culture may seem very distant from your situation. Yet in our hearts, each of us is like Jonah: We rebel against holiness. We resist compassion and grace. We remain distant from the God we claim to serve. Everyone in Jonah's story is in desperate need of heaven's mercy—including you, the reader.

BIBLE CONVERSATION *20 minutes*

In the lessons to come, you will be studying the book of Jonah piece by piece. But in this lesson, you will begin by getting an overview of the entire book and considering it as a whole. Have four volunteers **read all of Jonah aloud** for the group, each taking one chapter. Then discuss the questions below.

Most people think of the big fish when they think of the story of Jonah. What other important elements or themes do you notice that make this more than a fish story? In a few words, what is the book about?

Which of Jonah's behaviors or reactions feel familiar to you because you recognize them as being similar to your own behaviors and reactions? Explain.

****

In the article below, the author reflects on how Jonah's behaviors remind him of his own attitudes. Read it aloud, taking turns at the paragraph breaks.

CONFESSIONS OF A "GOOD" CHRISTIAN

5 minutes

Do good people really need grace? Many of us were brought up to think grace was for other people: those who had trampled on God's laws and ruined their lives and the lives of others. Grace was for people who slept around, had uncontrollable tempers, or abused drugs and alcohol. Why would good, church-attending, Bible-believing, law-keeping Christians need grace?

Of course, we made *mistakes*, or sometimes even messed up. But we expected God to forgive us for those minor peccadillos because—well, the rest of our lives were pretty much under control, so why wouldn't he? I mean, otherwise who would be left to make up the numbers in his church? Certainly not those wild and rebellious sinners out there! Many of us grew up with a clear division of the world into good people and bad people. Bad people could become part of the church, provided they gave up being bad and became good like us. And good people had better not ever commit a Really Big Mistake, because that might ruin everything.

Of course, one problem with this world view is the surprising reluctance of our own hearts to fall into line. Outwardly, we might be able to meet the expected standards of righteousness. Most of the time we might not say out loud what we are thinking about others (at least not to their faces), but what are we thinking? Inside we still struggle with a hidden cesspool of anger, bitterness, lust, pride, jealousy, and assorted other sins.

Recently, I have been struck by my own self-righteousness in response to the news of a well-known pastor who committed adultery. My outward, "correct" response was: *I could do that too. Thank you, Lord, for your grace, which is the only thing that keeps me safe.* But I showed an inner condemnation of him in how critical I was of his subsequent words and actions. I expected him to respond perfectly to a situation in which his whole world must have been falling apart. Like Jonah, I had no compassion on him.

The result of this perspective is a world divided into black and white, with us clearly on the side of the angels. We may speak of grace in precise theological terms, but we are never really astonished by it. It is there for bad people who really need it, but we don't personally have much use for it. As a result, we sometimes have a problem with how freely God seems to dole it out. In principle, we might be comfortable with the idea of bad people receiving grace—but not when their sins make people think badly about the church, or hurt us deeply and personally.

The book of Jonah was written for people like us. In it, we see God do some astonishing things. There is the huge fish that swallows Jonah, of course, and the luxuriant plant that sprouts in the desert. Even more remarkable is the totally unexpected repentance of a group of hardened sailors, and the repentance of an entire city after probably the shortest and worst evangelistic outreach in history. Yet the central focus is the Lord's unrelenting pursuit of Jonah, the self-righteous prophet, who flings Scripture back in God's face to justify his anger.

Perhaps you are familiar with Jesus's parable about the prodigal son (Luke 15:11–32). That story does not conclude with the wayward son's return but shifts focus to the heart of the elder brother. So too, the book of Jonah shows us an angry believer who would rather die than see God's grace extended to the undeserving. In the prodigal son story, one amazing element is the Father leaving his son's welcome home party to search for the lost elder brother. He too must be brought back for the celebration to be complete.

Here is great news for self-righteous elder brothers like me: The Good Shepherd is not just seeking the wandering sheep who have strayed into a far country; he is seeking the sheep who are proud of the fact they stayed home. The Great Physician not only has a cure for those who know their disease to be terminal but he also has the remedy for those who dismiss their spiritual malady as a mere sniffle. It is not an easy and painless cure. It involves opening our hearts up to public display and recognizing the truth about our inner selves. We are indeed much more sinful than we have ever dared to confess, perhaps even to ourselves.

All this the book of Jonah makes clear, yet it ends with an unanswered question. We never do hear the end of Jonah's story. The reason is simple: what counts today is not what Jonah decided to do, but what you will do with the Father's grace. Will it melt your icy heart, or will you remain stuck in your self-confident assertion that you don't really need it?

The gospel is, after all, not just the good news of forgiveness. It is also the announcement of a gift—the righteousness of Christ. This is the perfect righteousness God demands of us. Only this righteousness of Christ can finally give our frantic hearts the rest we so crave. And to receive this gift, we have to open our hands and let go of our efforts to prove ourselves worthy of God's love (our self-generated righteousness). I need to hear that message repeated regularly, and so do you—especially if you are one of the good people.

DISCUSSION *10 minutes*

Do you tend to think of yourself as one of the bad people or as one of the good people? Explain why.

The article mentions being searched out by God, opening your heart to public display, and recognizing the truth about yourself—all of which will be part of the coming lessons! What about this feels inviting to you, and what feels uncomfortable? Again, explain why.

EXERCISE

JOYS AND TRIALS

15 minutes

The book of Jonah is about a series of events—pleasant and troubling, big and small—in the prophet's life. They are events arranged by God to teach Jonah about his heart and bring him closer to God. So, studying Jonah will include examining the events in your life and thinking about how God has used them to do the same. Sharing some of this with the group will also help you get to know one another better.

Begin on your own. Read the statements below about the joys and trials God has put in your life. Consider how you would complete the sentences. When you're finished, you'll discuss them as a group.

JOYS

Something in my life that has made me very happy is

_____ .

A little thing in my life that always gives me joy is

_____ .

One thing I've learned about myself, by considering what makes me happy, is

_____ .

One thing God has taught me about himself, through his grace in my life, is

_____ .

TRIALS

A particularly difficult trial in my life was/is

_____ .

A little thing that always irks me or makes me sad is

_____ .

One thing I've learned about myself, by considering my trials and what makes me angry or sad, is

_____ .

One thing God has taught me about himself, through the trials in my life, is

_____ .

Now share some of your findings with the group. If you notice any pattern in how God deals with you, tell about that.

WRAP-UP AND PRAYER *5 minutes*

As with Jonah's story, your story is not about what you achieve on your own but rather God working through you and in you. Use your remaining time to pray together. Ask God to work in you through your study of Jonah, bringing you closer to him.

Lesson

2

RUNNING FROM GOD

BIG IDEA

Life's disappointments often distance us from God. We become angry or discouraged because he has not given us what we wanted. Yet this very frustration may be the means by which the Lord gives us what he wants, which is so much better.

BIBLE CONVERSATION *15 minutes*

Jonah had already served as the Lord's prophet before the book of Jonah begins. He had spoken of the Lord's undeserved grace to his home nation, the northern kingdom of Israel. King Jeroboam II was sinful and idolatrous, and yet the Lord sent Jonah to him with a surprising message of compassion and deliverance. Have someone in your group **read 2 Kings 14:23–27 aloud**.

In the book of Jonah, though, the message Jonah is sent to convey is not for Israel, but for Nineveh, the capital of the Assyrians, a traditional enemy of Israel. The Assyrians were notoriously brutal warriors, who regularly flayed their enemies alive, or cut off their lips or their heads. There was plenty of wickedness in Nineveh for the Lord to judge. **Read chapter 1 of Jonah aloud**, and then discuss the following questions.

Compared to his earlier work, how might Jonah feel about his new assignment to go to Nineveh? Discuss considerations such as safety, job satisfaction, potential rewards, popularity, et cetera.

Once the Lord sends the storm, does Jonah change his attitude or does he continue to "run" from God's command? Explain your answer.

Compare Jonah with the sailors. How are they different in their knowledge about God, and how are they different in their responsiveness to God? Which can you identify with?

＊＊＊＊

When we sin, we imagine it will bring us safety and satisfaction. But instead, as with Jonah, it always leads to some form of death. Read the article "Why We Run" aloud, taking turns at the paragraph breaks.

ARTICLE

WHY WE RUN

5 minutes

Although the book of Jonah starts with the Lord declaring the evil of Nineveh has come up before him, the bulk of the story is more concerned about an evil prophet. Jonah is surrounded by creatures that run to do the Lord's will—a fish, a plant, a worm, a wind, pagan sailors, and cruel Ninevites. Only Jonah stands against God and against grace, ready to die rather than relent. Jonah's evil is subtle and deep-rooted; healing him will be a delicate task.

Instead of going east to Nineveh, Jonah found a ship and fled about as far west as you could possibly go, to Tarshish. As William Banks puts it, "When a person decides to run from the Lord, Satan always provides complete transportation facilities."* Even in the storm, face-to-face with the reality of the Lord's judgment, Jonah preferred to hide. What's more, his willingness to be thrown overboard for the sake of the sailors may sound quite noble until you realize that in doing this, Jonah would still achieve his goal of frustrating the Lord's plans. He might die, but he would not deliver God's message to Nineveh.

In chapter 4:2, Jonah explains why he ran from God. He wasn't afraid of danger or failure in Nineveh; he was afraid of success. He feared that if he preached the Lord's message, the people would repent and escape God's judgment. Why should those brutal people receive grace

---

* William Banks, *Jonah: The Reluctant Prophet* (Chicago: Moody, 1966), 20.

so easily? Yet Jonah's problem was not ultimately with the Ninevites, but with God. Jonah quit and ran away from God because the Lord violated his sense of what kind of God he should be.

This is the same reason we turn our backs on God. Perhaps right now you are disappointed with the circumstances of your life. God has not given you the job, or the spouse, or the child you wanted—he has not been, for you, the God you think he should be. We typically respond to these disappointments in one of two ways: we live in denial and pretend all is fine, or we give up on God answering our prayers. Either approach means running away from a real relationship with God. In a real relationship, we must actually interact with the God who stubbornly refuses to conform to our wonderful plan for life but has his own—often more painful—plan for us.

For some of us, it is not so much our circumstances that frustrate us as our lack of holy living. You struggle with ongoing sin, which ties you in knots and hurts you and those around you. You have prayed and prayed for the Lord to take it away, but so far he has not seen fit to do so. How will you respond?

Again, your struggle is not merely with your sin; it is with God. That is why in the midst of our sin we often distance ourselves from God. I see this dynamic in my own heart as I wrestle with pride and self-centeredness. I pray for the Lord to change me, but I hate it when he actually confronts my sin. I bristle and resent it when other people point out my pride. I want to be fixed, but without actually having to be exposed and repent. So I find myself withdrawing, running from God.

Jonah's example shows that when we run from God, we go downward and inward. From the mountains of Israel, Jonah goes down to Joppa on the coast, then down into the inner part of the ship, and finally down into the depths of the sea itself. His physical movements parallel his spiritual journey away from the Lord. Moreover, his journey is inward, away from people as well as from God. He cuts himself off from his home and family, and even onboard ship he isolates himself from others and their needs.

This is what running from God does in our lives as well. We may still be Christians on the outside, answering the questions of those around us with a theologically correct, "I fear the Lord, the God of heaven." But in our hearts there is no affection, only a cold withdrawing into ourselves and away from God and others.

Yet the good news of the passage is that the Lord is in charge even of those who try to run from him. We need to nuance the earlier quote I cited: it was not ultimately Satan who provided the transport for Jonah, but God. The Lord provided the boat so Jonah could experience how the Lord is indeed the God "who made the sea." The Lord provided the storm so Jonah could see with crystal clarity that he could never get away from God. Even Jonah's attempt to end his own life could not succeed without the Lord's permission.

God doesn't even need our holiness to get his work done. Jonah was in no fit state to preach the gospel to anyone—he refused even to pray for the sailors—but the Lord saved them anyway! In the sovereignty of the Lord, Jonah's rebellion became the means for these sailors to experience the power of God and come to know him.

You will never outrun God or escape his perfect will for your life. Indeed, when you have run as far as you can, you will find that he has run further and is waiting there to greet you and show you the grace you have long resisted, to welcome you into his safe harbor in Christ. Here in this broken world, we continue to experience the storms of life, complete with rolling waves and fierce winds. Here our wicked and evil hearts continue to rebel and run away, as you and I have done repeatedly even this past week. Yet here too the Lord's grace is sufficient for us. And he has prepared a new world for us where our disappointment, grief, and fear will finally be gone, swallowed up in fullness, joy, and love. Stop running from him, and rest in that reality.

DISCUSSION *10 minutes*

Think about times when you don't want to be near to God, either because you don't like the life he has given you or you don't want to obey him. Why do you run and hide instead of admitting your struggles to God?

How do you feel about the way God kept pursuing, using, and teaching an obvious sinner like Jonah?

How might God flip your personal "Jonah story" around so instead of causing you to run from God, your disappointments and anger cause you to run to him?

LIFE ON THE RUN

15 minutes

In this exercise, you will chart in more detail what it looks like in your life to run from God. If you can, think of a way you have distanced yourself from God, perhaps by pretending everything is okay or by giving up on praying about something. Using that example, fill in the chart where applicable. When you are done, share some of your observations with the group.

1. I have avoided God because:

   ☐ I am angry at him about _____ .

   ☐ I am discouraged about _____ .

   ☐ I don't want to obey God about _____ .

   ☐ I don't want to be reminded of _____ .

   ☐ I'm just not interested. I care more about _____ .

   ☐ Other: _____ .

2. Instead of having a real relationship with God (which includes struggling to trust him when his plans are different from mine), I am tempted to treat him like:

   ☐ A lucky charm I carry around, hoping it might make things work out the way I want.

☐ A listening ear to whom I pour out my sorrows, as therapy.

☐ A multilane highway that ought to let me progress as a Christian without delays or detours.

☐ A rulebook to follow, within reason.

☐ Other: _____ .

3. I have gone *downward* and *inward* by becoming like:

☐ A turtle, hiding from God and others inside my shell.

☐ A spiky hedgehog, prickly when God or others come near.

☐ A stubborn mule, doing whatever I want even when faced with God's truth.

☐ A sloth, intending to draw nearer to God . . . someday . . . soon.

☐ A puppy, wearing a happy face no matter what.

☐ Other: _____ .

4. In spite of my coldness toward him, God has pursued me by:

☐ Sending a "storm" in the form of _____ .

☐ Reminding me of the truth that _____ .

☐ Showing me mercy and kindness by _____ .

☐ Other: _____ .

5. I am most encouraged to come near to God by the good news that:

☐ God's sovereign care for me does not stop even when I try to run from him.

☐ God is in control of the storms of life, and he will use them for my good.

☐ God is not shocked by my sin; he is waiting at the end of my run to show me the grace I have resisted.

☐ God has prepared a new home for me where my disappointment, grief, and fear will one day be gone.

☐ Other: _____ .

WRAP-UP AND PRAYER

Most of us find it intensely hard to trust God when he tells us to do something that makes our skin crawl. Yet this is how we truly fear the Lord and accept he is God. And our frustration with his choices may be the means by which he gives us what he wants for us, which is so much better.

Spend your remaining time praying together that God would help you draw near to him in all situations—which is the best gift of all.

3

REDEEMING THE RUNAWAYS

BIG IDEA

The book of Jonah tells us, "Salvation belongs to the Lord!" (2:9). Jonah is a sign that points ahead to a better prophet—our only Savior, Jesus.

BIBLE CONVERSATION *20 minutes*

In this lesson, you will start looking ahead to the New Testament to see Jonah's story in terms of what Jesus has done for you. If some in your group missed the last lesson, or if you want a reminder of what happened in the first chapter of Jonah, **begin by reading chapter 1 of Jonah aloud** again.

Jonah points ahead to several events in Jesus's life. One with interesting parallels happened when Jesus and his disciples were at the Sea of Galilee. Have someone **read that account aloud from Mark 4:35–41**. Then discuss the questions below.

Both events include a boat, a life-threatening storm, and a sleeping man of God. But how are Jesus's actions and demeanor in the storm different from Jonah's? List several differences.

Jesus suggests the lesson learned from the storm is we should have faith. Why do you think he mentions faith at such a time?

One other event happened late in Jesus's life on earth, in the garden of Gethsemane, the night before he completed the Father's assignment to die on the cross for our sin. That time the roles were reversed: Jesus was awake and troubled, while his disciples slept. Have someone **read Luke 22:39–46 aloud**. Then discuss the questions below.

****

The article "Into the Storm" will show you some ways Jonah points to Jesus. Read it aloud, taking turns at the paragraph breaks.

Lesson

3

ARTICLE

INTO THE STORM

5 minutes

What should we do with evil people? Some of us would like to put them in jail and throw away the key. Others want to show compassion, seeking to understand their hurts and pain. The book of Jonah is about what to do with evil people, but not quite how you might expect. We might better ask the question this way: What does God do with rebellious runaways like Jonah and like us?

Salvation clearly is not going to come through the prophet or any mere human. Jesus said Jonah was a sign, pointing to him. Salvation has come to us only because the Lord turned the sign that was Jonah into the reality that is Jesus. In place of a rebellious prophet, he sent the ultimate obedient prophet to redeem runaways like us. In future lessons we'll see many ways Jesus fulfills the sign of Jonah, but here I want to focus on just three.

First, there is the contrast between Jonah's flight and Jesus's faithfulness. Jonah was judgmental and without compassion, and so he fled rather than extend grace to Ninevites he deemed unworthy. But Jesus did the opposite: rather than judge hardened sinners and flee from them, he went to the cross to rescue them. He resolutely set his face and traveled toward Jerusalem, a city that would not repent even when the Son of God himself visited—a city that would kill him. Jesus could have judged those people, but instead he wept over them with deep compassion and love, humbling himself profoundly among them (see Luke 19:41–44).

Second, the book of Jonah is read in the Jewish tradition as part of the liturgy of the Day of Atonement. One biblical instruction for that day tells the high priest to take two goats and cast lots over them. One goat was singled out to die while the other was driven into the wilderness (Leviticus 16:8–10).* These scapegoats bore the sins of the community and atoned for those sins by death and banishment. Jonah is a sort of scapegoat too, but a very imperfect one: his journey into the darkness and his selection by lot to die came with sinful motives. The true scapegoat is Jesus, the Lamb of God who takes away our sin. He freely took the role of both goats—dying for sin and bearing the separation from God that sin brings—to bring us back into the presence of the Father.

Third, there is the incident in Mark 4, where the disciples were caught in a great storm on the Sea of Galilee while Jesus slept in the boat. Notice what Jesus did when he was awakened. He didn't merely pray to the Lord to still the storm; he spoke directly to the storm and quieted it with a word. He is God himself, with complete control over the circumstances around him. This merely heightens the intensity of the other instance in which Jesus faced a storm, in the garden of Gethsemane. There he faced an oncoming outburst of God's wrath that would be poured out upon him—not for any sin of his own, but for the sin of his people. Jesus had every right to run from that assignment. The sin was not his, but ours. Yet he did not flee. He bowed his head and said, "Not my will but yours be done."

Yes, Jesus was willing to die if that's what it meant to say *not my will but yours be done*. What a contrast with Jonah, who preferred to die rather than say yes to God's will! Surely you too have found yourself unwilling to say yes to God—unwilling to accept his will in your life circumstances, your relationships, or your sanctification. But Jesus said it in your place, and then he died in your place. Jesus never turned or fled from the Father, and yet the Father thrust him away as distantly

---

* See Janet Howe Gaines, *Forgiveness in a Wounded World: Jonah's Dilemma* (Atlanta: Society of Biblical Literature, 2003), 148.

as if he had gone to hell itself. Jesus took the judgment you deserve, to bring salvation to a rebellious runaway. He could have stilled that storm as easily as he did the earlier one on the Sea of Galilee, but for your sake he went into the heart of it.

This is the love as vast as the ocean Jonah tried to cross, the love that calls you into a relationship with the Lord as your heavenly Father. Perhaps it is calling to you for the first time, like those pagan sailors who glimpsed the intensity of the Lord's power in that storm. Come like them today and drop to your knees, marveling at this God who not only created the sea and the dry land, but cares intensely for the creatures he has made.

For others, this love woos you out of repeated rebellion and a heart that's frustrated with God. Come and see how much he has loved you. Will your Father give you a stone when you ask for bread? Surely, he will give you good things, even if you cannot understand yet how these challenging circumstances, or difficult relationships, or besetting sins will work for good in your life. Sometimes, God may miraculously quiet the storm around you. At other times, he may quiet your heart in the midst of a storm that continues to rage. Yet he will always be with you, at work when your heart is soft and when it is hard, shaping and molding you through various trials, until he completes the good work he has begun in you.

DISCUSSION *10 minutes*

Why might hard times and difficult commands work for your good? Think of several reasons.

Although Jesus didn't face hard times due to his own sin (he didn't have any sin!), he did allow himself to suffer due to our sin and the condition of this world. How is the fact that Jesus suffered a help to you when you struggle with hard times or sin? Again, think of several reasons.

THE STORMS OF LIFE

20 minutes

Jonah's story can help us see three ways we might respond to the storms of life. Each can take several possible outward forms.

The **SCRAMBLING SAILOR** response

- You start rowing as hard as you can. You rely on your strength and do everything in your power to overcome the problem.

- You cry out to your gods. You turn to anyone and anything you can think of—money, experts, doctors, friends, family members, people who owe you favors, your reputation around town—in the hope that one of these can save you.

- You throw your cargo overboard. You try to get rid of bad habits, sinful baggage, and wrong influences in the hope that straightening out your life will solve your problem or earn you God's favor.

The **SLEEPING JONAH** response

- You hide below deck. You rebel and withdraw, hardening your heart against God and those around you. Or you pretend your problem isn't really a problem at all, and everything is manageable.

- You go to sleep. You know there's a problem but you try to forget about it. Thinking about it is too stressful or challenges you in ways you would rather avoid.

- You give up on God. You might keep talking *about* him, but you seldom pray to him about your problem because you are too proud, you don't believe God will listen to someone like you, or because praying about it might mean you also have to accept God's answer to it.

The **PERSON OF FAITH** response

- You turn toward God instead of away from him. Like a child, you trust your Father with whatever he wants for you, caring more that he is with you than about the circumstances surrounding you.

- You grab onto Jesus. You know life will include huge storms, but you are encouraged by God's promises to be good to you, which are your "sure and steadfast anchor of the soul" (Hebrews 6:19).

- You cry out to your Savior and hear him say, "Peace! Be still!" You find strength in God—knowing you are his forgiven child, and in his good time he is making you holy and bringing you into eternal life with him.

Most of us have some mixture of all these responses. Think about how you usually respond to hard times and disappointments, and then select the mix that best fits what you tend to do.

In hard times, I respond like a **SCRAMBLING SAILOR**:

- ☐ Almost always
- ☐ Most of the time
- ☐ Sometimes
- ☐ Seldom
- ☐ Almost never

In hard times, I respond like a **SLEEPING JONAH**:

    ☐ Almost always

    ☐ Most of the time

    ☐ Sometimes

    ☐ Seldom

    ☐ Almost never

In hard times, I respond like a **PERSON OF FAITH**:

    ☐ Almost always

    ☐ Most of the time

    ☐ Sometimes

    ☐ Seldom

    ☐ Almost never

Many of us respond one way to hard times that aren't our fault, but somewhat differently when our problem is with ongoing sin or a struggle to obey God. So now, fill in the chart a second time to reflect how you deal with sin in your life.

Faced with my sin, I respond like a **SCRAMBLING SAILOR**:

    ☐ Almost always

    ☐ Most of the time

    ☐ Sometimes

    ☐ Seldom

    ☐ Almost never

Faced with my sin, I respond like a **SLEEPING JONAH**:

☐ Almost always

☐ Most of the time

☐ Sometimes

☐ Seldom

☐ Almost never

Faced with my sin, I respond like a **PERSON OF FAITH**:

☐ Almost always

☐ Most of the time

☐ Sometimes

☐ Seldom

☐ Almost never

Now share some of your observations with the group. If you found your approach to overcoming sin is different from your approach to other hard times, consider why this is so.

Scrambling sailor responses and sleeping Jonah responses are both self-focused, while faith is Christ-focused. Remember how the disciples were filled with awe when they saw Jesus calm the storm. What awe-instilling truths about Jesus do you hope to see more clearly as a help to live by faith?

WRAP-UP AND PRAYER *5 minutes*

When we see our need for faith, one of the best things to do is to go ahead and start practicing faith immediately, by praying. So, use the rest of your time praying together. You might want to pray for faith itself—that God would help you turn to him in all your struggles.

4

SALVATION IS OF THE LORD

BIG IDEA

Whether you have given yourself over to your sin, run away from God, or become puffed up in pride for *not* doing these things, your only hope is in the truth that salvation is of the Lord.

BIBLE CONVERSATION *20 minutes*

Chapter 2 of Jonah consists mostly of the prophet's prayer from inside the fish. The prayer takes the form of a psalm of acknowledgment, which is a kind of psalm used regularly in Israel to recognize and give thanks to the Lord for deliverance from trouble. Jonah's psalm has several parts:

- The opening verse summarizes Jonah's trouble and the Lord's deliverance. (In the ancient world, *Sheol* was the home of the dead.)
- The next section chronicles Jonah's descent into this watery hell.
- Then we hear how the Lord rescued Jonah.
- Finally, Jonah expresses a few lessons that should be learned from his experience.

Have someone in the group **read chapter 2 of Jonah aloud**. Then discuss the questions below.

How would you briefly describe Jonah's downward journey? What types of depth did he experience? What was it like for him emotionally?

Based on verses 7–9, what lessons do you think Jonah learned from his experience? How do these compare to what God has taught you by allowing hard times in your life?

Is anything missing from this prayer? What else might you like to see from Jonah that would show you he's really been changed by his experience of grace?

****

Several lines in the psalm mention how God controlled Jonah's situation. Read aloud the article "God in Charge," taking turns at the paragraph breaks.

Lesson

ARTICLE

GOD IN CHARGE

5 minutes

When the sailors tossed Jonah overboard, he must have thought it was the end of his life. At least he wouldn't have to go and preach to Nineveh. But throughout the Jonah narrative, the Lord's sovereignty repeatedly trumps Jonah's rebellion. God's plans always succeed, and this in itself should be an encouraging word to all of us. As Jonah himself proclaimed, "Salvation belongs to the Lord!" (2:9).

Do you imagine you have messed up God's plan for your life, perhaps through sinful choices? The book of Jonah shows how the Lord is in charge over that. His sovereign will to deal with Jonah's heart is the key element in this story, and he works all things together to accomplish that wonderful end. It will be the same for you. The Lord has brought you where you are today for a reason. And as you turn to him in faith, he will use even the sins and the trials that feel so devastating to bring good fruit in your life.

Notice the Lord's patience in showing grace to Jonah and giving him a second chance. Jonah's cry from the belly of the fish shows you can never be too far gone to cry out to the Lord. At the very moment that seems blackest and most hopeless, the Lord has you exactly where he wants you—at the place where nothing and no one but him can possibly help you. He will not turn your cry away because you are a sinner, or because you are utterly lost. After all, Jesus Christ came to rescue sinners and "to seek and to save the lost" (Luke 19:10). He will hear you and answer you in the way that is best for you.

So, what does Jonah say to the Lord, and what does his psalm tell us about his heart? Certainly, Jonah is changing, finally praying to the Lord. Yet as the story unfolds in chapters 3 and 4, it will become clear Jonah's attitude toward the Ninevites hasn't really changed at all. And if you read this psalm closely, I think you can see why. Notice Jonah's prayer includes no acknowledgment of his own sin. In fact, Jonah almost makes himself sound like an innocent bystander. He claims, "I am driven away from your sight," but fails to mention how he was the one who fled from the Lord in the first place.

This lack of repentance is perhaps most evident in the teaching section at the end of the psalm. Here Jonah contrasts "those who pay regard to vain idols" with himself—"But I with the voice of thanksgiving will sacrifice to you; what I have vowed I will pay" (2:9). It seems he is thinking of people like the Ninevites or the sailors as pagan outsiders who have no covenantal claim on the Lord's steadfast love, while good Israelites like him are insiders who may surely experience that love and mercy even when they stray.

The result of this perspective was that Jonah magnified the sins of others and minimized his own sin. The irony is the pagan sailors (the outsiders) had actually offered sacrifices and made vows to the Lord at the end of chapter 1, while Jonah (the insider who speaks about those things with all the right theology) was submerged under the waves. Perhaps it is little wonder that at the end of Jonah's psalm the fish vomited him out onto the dry ground. It seems the fish could not stomach him any longer.

This means Jonah is not an example of how we *should* behave, but a picture of how we often do behave. A truly correct theology would remind us that none of us is an insider to grace: we are all amazed guests at the table of the Lord's mercy. But like Jonah, we too divide the world into insiders and outsiders. For myself, I often live in a state of denial over sin. There is little confession of sin in my prayers, and as a result I don't find God's grace to me all that amazing. Others struggle with the opposite side of the same confusion. They feel that because of their sins and struggles they cannot possibly be an insider, a welcome member of the family of God.

Whichever side of the truth you are inclined to fall off on, the answer is contained in the glorious theological statement Jonah uttered but didn't really grasp: Salvation is of the Lord. He is sovereign over our salvation from beginning to end. That means if I am part of God's chosen people, it is not because I am a particularly "choice" person. It is by grace alone and not of works, as Ephesians 2:8 puts it, so no one can boast.

Equally, if salvation is of the Lord from beginning to end, it is not something I can lose through my sin and failure. Jonah's life was full of unconfessed sin and rank rebellion, yet the Lord didn't wait to see if Jonah would cry out from the deep before he appointed a fish to rescue him. It is the same when anyone comes to faith in Christ. No one is saved without that cry of faith, yet the Lord is sovereign over all the circumstances that make you first cry out to him, and then he is also in charge of maintaining your salvation. It does not depend on your ability to keep yourself from idolatry—far from it; even when we outwardly obey God we often do so with selfish pride or mixed motives. Rather, in spite of our constant idolatry, the Lord's steadfast love remains equally sure. He will keep you safe to the end of your spiritual journey here on earth.

DISCUSSION *10 minutes*

It's easy to be astonished at Jonah's ability to ignore and rationalize away his own heart rebellion, but how do you often do the same thing?

How do you imagine God interacts with your spiritual growth? Do you imagine him beaming with pride because of your progress? Actively involved? Sitting back and wondering if you will ever improve?

Lesson

EXERCISE

INSIDERS AND OUTSIDERS

15 minutes

The article mentioned two ways we can miss the truth that salvation belongs to the Lord: (1) we might imagine we are entitled insiders, or (2) we might feel like unwelcome outsiders. Look at the descriptions of how each kind of thinking might pop up in different areas of your Christian life and how they compare to the truth that salvation is of the Lord. Note thought processes that sound familiar to you, and then discuss the questions with your group.

APPROACH TO **PRAYER LIFE**

Insider thinking: Your prayers are more likely to mention the sins of others than confession of your own.

Outsider thinking: Your prayer life may be filled with lots of confession of sin, but you never feel as though you have confessed enough or that God has forgiven you and is now pleased with you.

Salvation is of the Lord: You are quick to confess your sin, and equally quick to enjoy your Father's forgiveness and welcome.

36

APPROACH TO **CHRISTIAN HERITAGE**

Insider thinking: You feel secure or superior because of your Christian family, good teaching you've received, or engrained moral habits.

Outsider thinking: You feel you've failed as a Christian because you haven't followed the good habits you've been taught.

Salvation is of the Lord: You look less at your own level of faithfulness, and more at the faithful Father who has brought you into his family to stay.

APPROACH TO **KNOWING THE TRUTH**

Insider thinking: You are proud of your correct theology, and quick to find flaws in the thinking of other Christians.

Outsider thinking: You may believe and spout all the right things about God, but you feel like a fake for not living up to your great theology.

Salvation is of the Lord: You appreciate what others bring to the body of Christ that you don't, and you trust God is in charge of each believer's growth—including yours.

APPROACH TO **SEEING YOUR SIN**

Insider thinking: You're glad you aren't one of those really bad sinners, and you expect God to forgive your faults because most of your life is pretty much under control.

Outsider thinking: You can't imagine God would ever have the patience to forgive you, since you continue to sin the same way again and again.

Salvation is of the Lord: When you see your sin you also see the perfect goodness of Christ, credited to you, which remains sufficient to save you in the end, just as it was when you first believed.

APPROACH TO **HARD TIMES OR CONSEQUENCES**

Insider thinking: You wonder how God could let such a thing happen to you.

Outsider thinking: You see consequences for sin as God's punishment rather than as helpful discipline from a Father who loves you.

Salvation is of the Lord: You expect God to use the hard times for your good, perhaps to draw you closer to him.

APPROACH TO **GOD'S FAVOR**

Insider thinking: Based on others you see, you're pretty sure you (or your church) must be one of God's favorites.

Outsider thinking: You think you might be tolerated for a while as a guest among the people of God, but you are convinced the moment will come when your true self will finally be exposed.

Salvation is of the Lord: You are amazed the Lord's grace is wide enough to encompass even someone like you.

APPROACH TO **YOUR FUTURE WITH GOD**

Insider thinking: You keep your sin hidden behind your religious rhetoric, speaking of salvation as if God owes it to you due to your faith.

Outsider thinking: You imagine God sitting in heaven—distant, disapproving, and doubtful about your chances of repenting so he can save you.

Salvation is of the Lord: You rejoice that God is with you and he knows exactly how he will complete your spiritual growth and salvation.

APPROACH TO **RELATIONSHIPS**

Insider thinking: You stay away from being friends with people who don't yet know Jesus, knowing how much sin is in their lives.

Outsider thinking: You are afraid to spend time with not-yet believers or share your faith with them—surely they'll just reject you or think of you as a "religious nut."

Salvation is of the Lord: You understand not-yet believers need the same thing you do—God's daily grace to redeem them. So you are willing to invite them to taste God's grace along with yourself.

Share some of what you learned about yourself: Are you more tempted to feel like an insider or an outsider? Which statements come especially close to the way you think? How would it help you to remember salvation is of the Lord?

WRAP-UP AND PRAYER *5 minutes*

Spend your remaining time praying together. You might want to include in your prayer some of the important things Jonah left out of his.

And if, like Jonah, you are at a particularly low point in your life, remember the Lord can and will help you when you cry out to him at that lowest point. Cry to him where you are and just as you are, and he will hear your cry and answer you from heaven.

5

FULL JUDGMENT, FULL SALVATION

BIG IDEA

Jonah's experience with the fish points to the greater prophet who came after him. Jesus received the full judgment of God, going down to the grave, and rose again to give us free and full salvation.

BIBLE CONVERSATION *20 minutes*

Jonah's descent into the fish and rescue from his watery grave isn't just a quirky tale told in the book of Jonah and then forgotten. Later in the Bible, Jesus mentioned it to some religious leaders who had accused him of doing his miracles in the devil's power rather than as a prophet from God. Have someone in the group **read Matthew 12:38–42 aloud**. Then discuss the questions.

If you wanted to mention a prophet who points ahead to Jesus, disobedient Jonah might seem like a poor choice. But what elements of Jonah's story make him a forerunner to Jesus's ministry? What does the fact that Jesus chose to mention Jonah say about Jesus's chief purpose while he was here on earth?

What is so compelling about the death and resurrection of Jesus that makes it the one sign by which we're called to repent and believe? Mention several aspects.

The religious leaders actually had no sincere interest in believing in Jesus, and even after he gave them his sign by rising from the dead they continued to oppose him (see Matthew 28:11–13). What can make people resistant to such great news as Jesus's death and resurrection?

****

One wonder of the cross is that by it God shows loving mercy to people who deserve nothing but judgment. Read aloud the article "Faithfulness to the Unfaithful," taking turns at the paragraph breaks.

ARTICLE

FAITHFULNESS TO THE UNFAITHFUL

5 minutes

We are so familiar with Jonah's story that it seems entirely natural to us for him to be safe inside the big fish. Allow yourself to be amazed by it afresh. Whoever heard of someone being swallowed by a fish and surviving? In antiquity, three days and three nights was how long it was thought to take to journey to Sheol, the dark home of the unquiet dead where those who rebel against God deserve to end up. Jonah described his place inside the fish as the belly of Sheol, the deepest and most enclosed part of that dismal dungeon. The fish could just as easily have vomited Jonah into hell as back onto dry land.

Then how is it possible the Lord showed such steadfast, covenant faithfulness to an unfaithful person like Jonah—or like us? The answer is found in the One to whom Jonah points, the prophet who is far better than Jonah. This final prophet had no personal sin of which he needed to repent and be washed clean, yet he identified with our sins in his baptism. That baptism was a sign both of God's watery judgment that washes sinners away like a flood, and of God's cleansing mercy that sprinkles our hearts with clean water and makes us clean.

Jonah saw outsiders as great sinners while failing to see he was a big sinner too. But Jesus, even though he was perfect with no sin of his own, didn't look down on those who were still mired in their own sin.

Far from excluding others as outsiders, Jesus welcomed the despised and the outcasts: He announced he was the Messiah to the woman of Samaria who had had multiple husbands and was part of an idolatrous people. He reached out to tax collectors and notorious sinners with the message they too could be saved.

What's more, Jesus constantly obeyed the will of his Father. He never once fled from the task assigned to him as Jonah did and as we do daily. Yet for him the path of obedience to the Father meant facing profound separation from him for our sins. Jesus went down past the gates of Sheol into hell itself on his three-day journey. He was driven away from the Father's presence into the utter aloneness of physical and spiritual death. He didn't just have a near-death experience as Jonah did; he actually died and felt the full measure of God's wrath against the sin of the covenant breakers with whom he was identifying—you and me.

That was Jesus's baptism of judgment that not only immersed him but dragged him down to its deepest depths. On the cross, God the Father did not reach down and deliver the life of his precious Son from the pit. When the Son uttered his agonized cry, "My God, my God why have you forsaken me," the Father did not craft some miraculous beast to rescue him from his peril. Instead, the Father turned out the lights on his obedient but desolated Son, leaving him in the thick darkness of death, closed off from light and life.

Yet that is not the end of the story. As Psalm 16:10 declares, the Lord would not finally abandon the soul of his Holy One in Sheol, nor let him see the pit. Jonah's deliverance was in its most profound sense a kind of dress rehearsal for Jesus's resurrection, as the sign of Jonah found its true fulfillment in Christ. And so, on the third day, Jesus rose again, triumphant over the tomb. The earth did not vomit him out. Rather, death simply could not hold Jesus, for he was innocent of sin. And so, he triumphed once and for all over sin and death and hell.

Because Christ showed such covenant faithfulness in suffering and dying for you, sacrificing himself in obedience to the Father's promise, now you can receive full and free salvation from the Lord. You and I can joyfully present our sacrifice of praise to Christ with thanksgiving, knowing nothing can now separate us from the loving presence of the Father—not even our ongoing idolatry and sin. God's steadfast love is ours in Christ. The Father will never leave us or forsake us.

Understanding this should give us great assurance in our salvation, and it should also prepare us to love and welcome other "great sinners" into the family of God. Can you look down on anyone else, no matter what they have done, once you have seen yourself as a great sinner? All of us are idolaters who have forfeited our right to the Lord's steadfast love. But even though we are all great sinners, Jesus Christ is a great Savior for great sinners.

This truth should then motivate us to go eagerly with the good news of the gospel to those who have not yet heard it, whether they are far from God like the Ninevites or outwardly upright, religious people like Jonah. Jesus rescues prodigal sons and elder brothers, despondent tax collectors and self-righteous Pharisees alike. He can and will deliver all those who cry out to him, who turn to him and his death on the cross as their only hope. The same grace he has offered to us he also offers to them—to deliver our souls from destruction and keep us safe from the pit, until we reach the solid ground of our eternal home.

DISCUSSION *10 minutes*

How has our study of Jonah so far helped you more deeply appreciate how you are a great sinner who has a great Savior?

The article mentioned three ways the good news of Jesus's death and resurrection might affect our hearts: (1) we can have joyful assurance we are saved, (2) we can welcome big sinners instead of looking down on them, and (3) we can be eager to tell all kinds of people about Jesus. Which of these does God seem to be working in your heart, or which do you hope to grow in?

EXERCISE

DEAD AND ALIVE IN CHRIST

15 minutes

Jesus's journey into death and out again is not about him alone. If you believe in him, you are joined with him in his death and resurrection. The Bible says a great many things about what this means for you. Read through the partial list below, noting how the Bible addresses your heart, and complete the statements that follow. Then discuss your findings with the group.

Because Jesus died and rose again for you . . .

Your guilt is erased.
No matter how you have sinned, you are set free from every curse and all condemnation you deserve from God.

> "Christ redeemed us from the curse of the law by becoming a curse for us" (Galatians 3:13).

You are counted righteous.
Your lasting legacy will not be your failures and sins, but the perfectly good record of Jesus, which he shares with you.

> "[Righteousness] will be counted to us who believe in him who raised from the dead Jesus our Lord, who was delivered up for our trespasses and raised for our justification" (Romans 4:24–25).

You are loved.
In every way you hunger for love, you are loved—without having to earn it, at great personal cost, and with perfect delight—by God himself.

> "God shows his love for us in that while we were still sinners, Christ died for us" (Romans 5:8).

You have a home with God.
Your enemy status is reversed, and your Father welcomes you into his family forever—a place where you belong, soon never to be lonely again.

> "But now in Christ Jesus you who once were far off have been brought near by the blood of Christ" (Ephesians 2:13).

You are given a new and better purpose.
You are set free from your suffocating obsession with yourself and are becoming a shining light with a new love for God and others.

> "He died for all, that those who live might no longer live for themselves but for him who for their sake died and was raised" (2 Corinthians 5:15).

Your conscience is finally clean.
Everything you've tried to do to make yourself acceptable to God, only to still feel condemned, is a burden now dissolved in the blood of Jesus.

> "How much more will the blood of Christ, who through the eternal Spirit offered himself without blemish to God, purify our conscience from dead works to serve the living God" (Hebrews 9:14).

You are not ruled by your temptations.
Everything that scares you—hard times, evil people, temptations that won't stop—is now powerless to do you lasting harm; Jesus has complete control over them all!

> "Present yourselves to God as those who have been brought from death to life, and your members to God as instruments for

righteousness. For sin will have no dominion over you" (Romans 6:13–14).

Your shame is turned to joy.
All your shame is covered and replaced with joy in Jesus, who is not ashamed to call you his brother or sister—he too has joy over you.

> "For the joy that was set before him [Jesus] endured the cross, despising the shame, and is seated at the right hand of the throne of God" (Hebrews 12:2).

Your death is turned to victory.
When it comes, your death will not be a punishment for sin; instead, it will bring your sinning to an end and bring you into eternal life.*

> "Whoever hears my word and believes him who sent me has eternal life. He does not come into judgment, but has passed from death to life" (John 5:24).

You are alive forever.
Already now you have a seat of honor in heaven; you are alive with Christ, and where he has gone you surely will follow.

> "For you have died, and your life is hidden with Christ in God. When Christ who is your life appears, then you also will appear with him in glory" (Colossians 3:3–4).

You are on the winning side.
You are a part of the great work in all of history: Jesus's ransom of his people in every nation of the world.

> "By your blood you ransomed people for God from every tribe and language and people and nation" (Revelation 5:9).

---

* See question and answer 42 of the Heidelberg Catechism, *The Heidelberg Catechism with Scripture Texts* (Grand Rapids, MI: Faith Alive, 1989), 64.

You are included in God's mission.
Once we have received Christ and have been adopted into God's family, we also have the joy of inviting others to join God's family.

> "Go therefore and make disciples of all nations, baptizing them in the name of the Father and of the Son and of the Holy Spirit, teaching them to observe all that I have commanded you. And behold, I am with you always, to the end of the age" (Matthew 29:19–20).

Now complete the following statements.

One of these truths that especially encourages me is

_____.

One truth I wasn't aware of before, or seldom think about, is

_____.

Remembering the truth that _____.
could be especially helpful in my Christian life because

_____.

Discuss your responses with your group, and share why you answered the way you did.

WRAP-UP AND PRAYER

You might like to include some thanksgiving in your prayer time, focusing on what God has given you through the death and resurrection of Jesus.

6

THE MOST DIFFICULT AREAS OF LIFE

BIG IDEA

God repeatedly pushes you back into the most difficult areas of your life, where you struggle to obey him and may often fail. He does this out of love: he is teaching you about your heart and drawing you nearer to himself.

BIBLE CONVERSATION *20 minutes*

One of the great clichés from the world of soccer is *it was a game of two halves*, meaning the two halves of the game were utterly different from each other. In a similar way, we might say Jonah is a book of two halves. Each includes God's call to Jonah and an interaction with those who are far from God, followed by Jonah's subsequent interaction with the Lord. The book invites us to ask how the two halves compare—and what the final score was.

Begin your study of the second half by having someone **read Jonah 3:1–5 aloud**. Then discuss the questions below.

What can we learn about God from the fact that he gave Jonah a second chance to obey? Include both observations about God that make you feel good about him and observations that might make you feel uneasy.

How does Jonah's response this time compare to his earlier response? How might it still fall short of the kind of response we'd like to see?

How does Jonah's interaction with God in this passage remind you of some of your own dealings with God?

✳✳✳✳

In pushing us into difficult areas, God is being good to us in ways that go far beyond merely testing our obedience. Read about this in the article "A Reluctant Prophet." Read it aloud, taking turns at the paragraph breaks.

Lesson

ARTICLE

A RELUCTANT PROPHET

5 minutes

It should astound you that the Word of the Lord came a second time to Jonah. He didn't deserve a second chance, nor did he particularly want one. But the Lord called him to go to Nineveh once again. This shows God's mercy to those who fail and sin, which differs from how *we* typically respond when people let us down. If they are our employees, we fire them. If they are our families, we yell and scream, or we withdraw in cold silence, or we store up the incident to use against the offender for years to come. But God is not like us. He is loving and patient, the God of second chances.

Yet we should also recognize that this is not an absolute principle in the Bible. There are times when there are no second chances for the servants of God. This means we have to ask why the Lord gives Jonah another chance here. The answer is the Lord is once again deliberately confronting Jonah with his worst nightmare: calling him to obey in the most difficult area of his life. In his faithful pursuit of Jonah's heart, the Lord brings him back into precisely the same circumstances where he failed before.

Have you ever felt the Lord doing that with you? You have an area of sin or struggle, and instead of the Lord safely steering you away from temptation, he pushes you right back into that area. Sometimes I feel that way about church planting and pastoring. There are many things I love about it, but it exposes my sins and weaknesses far more obviously than being a seminary professor does.

As a professor, I can shut myself up with my nice and safe books and emerge at regular intervals to pontificate like an expert. But as a pastor, I'm supposed to love and care for people—even the ones who are hard to love. I'm supposed to notice when the sheep are hurting, wandering, or in trouble. And I often don't do that. I'm self-absorbed, and people often go unnoticed and unappreciated, which hurts the church and exposes my sinful heart. Yet time and time again, I find myself propelled by the Lord back into another church plant. The result will inevitably be more mess and more sin on my part.

Why does God do that with us? Why does he send us right back into areas that expose our sin? I'd be very happy for the Lord to instantly make me a better person and a better pastor so I love people well all the time. But he doesn't appear to have chosen that option. God delights in working not merely with weak people, but with broken and seriously deformed people. In that way, it becomes evident that the work is entirely his, not ours. When God uses us in spite of our terrible attitudes and uncaring selfishness, what can we say except salvation is of the Lord?

But there is another reason as well. We are not merely tools God uses to achieve his goals; we ourselves are people in whom God is at work. The Lord brings us into areas that expose our weakness, brokenness, and foul sin to show us the wickedness that remains in our hearts. Remember how Jonah already had a successful mission as a prophet in Israel. Maybe his success went to his head and made him feel as if he was something special. If so, his experience with the Ninevites was going to challenge that: Jonah promptly failed again.

To be sure, on this second occasion Jonah obeyed the Lord's call and went to Nineveh. Yet his actions upon arriving there suggest he was still far from being entirely on board with the mission. He went just one-third of the way into the city and cried out possibly the briefest and most obscure message in all of prophetic history—a mere five words in Hebrew. The kings and nobles of Nineveh were apparently not even aware of his visit until news reached them by way of the common people. By then, it seems Jonah had already left town.

Jonah was told to cry out the exact message the Lord told him to say, yet we are left wondering whether he actually did so. He doesn't even mention the Lord as the God from whom judgment is coming, and he says nothing about the possibility of repentance and grace. If Jonah had been confronted over his message, he doubtless would have responded by saying he had done what the Lord commanded him. But the way in which he did it reveals the hardness of his heart.

Aren't we often like Jonah in this? Our lack of love for others is exposed in the careless way in which we fulfill our mandate from the Lord to bring them the good news of salvation. We either don't bother to share the gospel with them at all, or if we do, we are motivated primarily by pride or guilt, so we leave satisfied if we have "done our duty" and spoken the truth—uncaring about whether we have presented it in the best possible way to communicate God's undying love for sinful people. Likewise, we can easily point out when someone else's painful circumstances are the result of their sin or irresponsibility, but we are not equally good at speaking grace and showing them the way back to the Lord through repentance and faith. We waltz into someone else's difficult situation, pronounce judgment on them, and waltz right out again when God's grace in our own life should prompt us to apply the same generous gospel to those who have wronged and hurt us.

Of course, we don't all sin in quite the same way Jonah did. Sometimes instead of resenting a second chance, we beg God for another opportunity to obey, confidently proclaiming we will do it right this time. Yet often we are not seeking a second chance out of a humble desire to serve others but out of a proud desire to prove to God we can succeed. If that is our motive, our "obedience" may be done in such a self-justifying way that it barely qualifies as obedience at all.

God is not just saving others, he is saving *you*. And that salvation process includes sanctification, which involves teaching you about your heart. If he has chosen and called you, he will not give you up. He is at work in you and will complete that great work on the last day. Let that reality encourage your heart before God today and soften it toward others around you.

DISCUSSION *10 minutes*

When life is easy, most of our inner depravity remains hidden from us. How have you learned about your heart from times God pushed you into difficult areas of life?

Motives matter, even when we outwardly say yes to God. Instead of obeying out of a *humble desire* to serve God and others, we may instead obey out of (1) a *prideful desire* to prove how godly we can be, or (2) a *guilt-ridden desire* to feel better about ourselves or avoid God's anger. Which of these self-focused motives tempts you, and why?

Lesson

EXERCISE

LOOK AT YOUR HEART

15 minutes

For this exercise, first think of a type of situation in which God has repeatedly placed you even though you tend to fail and to sin in that situation. For example, think of a way to serve the church or others that keeps popping up in your life even though it's not how you are "gifted." Or think of a difficult temptation that keeps coming back. (If you can't think of something you want to discuss with the group, just use *tell others about Jesus*. Most of us have some struggles in that area, as Jonah did.)

God repeatedly calls me to _____ . despite how I fail and sin in that situation.

God is teaching you about your heart, so let's think about that. When you realize God again wants you to do the thing you have failed at, what heart attitudes do you have?

- ☐ **Resentment.** "Again? This isn't fair!"

- ☐ **Fear.** "One way or another, this will turn out badly."

- ☐ **Coldness.** "I don't care what God says—nor do I care about others, really."

- ☐ **Stubbornness.** "Um, Lord, that's not how I'm gifted."

- ☐ **Denial.** "What do you mean, *fail*? I did okay last time."

- ☐ **Spiritual pride.** "Watch this, Lord. I'm going to do better this time!"

- ☐ **Spiritual worry.** "I *need* to do better this time or God will hate me."

- ☐ **Defeat.** "Why should I even bother this time?"

- ☐ **Half-heartedness.** "Well, I guess I can do some of that, this once."

- ☐ **Hiding.** "Hmm, how do I make sure no one sees how hard this is for me?"

- ☐ **Avoidance.** "I'm sure I'll get around to that once the Lord works on my heart a little more."

- ☐ **Self-condemnation.** "I feel like scum already."

- ☐ **Other.** _____ .

The writer of Hebrews quotes a proverb to remind us that God has a loving purpose behind these difficult areas of life: he is training us, Father to child.

> Have you forgotten the exhortation that addresses you as sons?
> "My son, do not regard lightly the discipline of the Lord
> nor be weary when reproved by him.
> For the Lord disciplines the one he loves,
> and chastises every son whom he receives."
> It is for discipline that you have to endure. God is treating you as sons. (Hebrews 12:5–7)

This passage says when we get weary from failure, we should remember how our struggles confirm the love, dignity, and protection we have as children of God. This brings new heart attitudes. Which new attitudes has God given you, or which do you hope for?

☐ **Belonging.** "This is how my Father is pursuing my heart. He loves me."

☐ **Contentment.** "One way or another, this will turn out for my good."

☐ **Dependence.** "I'll do this *with* God, not as a performance *for* God."

☐ **Prayerfulness.** "I really need your help here, Lord."

☐ **Teachability.** "I wonder what God wants me to learn through this."

☐ **Godly comfort.** "I'm safe! Failure can't destroy me because Jesus has saved me."

☐ **Confidence.** "My Father is determined to complete my salvation, and he's doing just that!"

☐ **Humility.** "I still have much to learn."

☐ **Worship.** "God is so beyond me!"

☐ **Faith.** "God isn't just *the* Father, he's *my* Father. He's bringing me closer to himself."

☐ **Other.** _____ .

Share some of your findings with the group. What do you think God is teaching you about your heart? If you had greater joy in the love, dignity, and protection you have as God's child, how might that change things?

WRAP-UP AND PRAYER

Use your remaining time to pray together. As you pray for hard situations in your life, pray both that God would help you obey him and that he would draw you closer to him along the way.

7

A CALL TO REPENT

BIG IDEA

The people of Nineveh responded to God with extraordinary repentance, and you have even more reason than they did to turn from sin and toward God.

BIBLE CONVERSATION *20 minutes*

The second half of Jonah 3 describes how the Ninevites repented. Repentance is a sorrow for sin and change of heart by which you turn away from evil, idols, and self-reliance, and declare that you will seek to move instead toward God in the future. Have someone **read all of Jonah 3 aloud**. Then discuss the following questions.

How is the repentance of the Ninevites full and deep rather than partial and shallow (think of several ways)? What evidence do you see that their repentance came from the heart?

What does the fact that God decided to work repentance in an evil city like Nineveh say about God's character? What does it suggest about his plan for the world?

In Exodus 34:7–8, the Lord describes himself as both merciful and a God who always punishes sin: "The LORD, the LORD, a God merciful and gracious, slow to anger, and abounding in steadfast love and faithfulness, keeping steadfast love for thousands, forgiving iniquity and transgression and sin, but who will by no means clear the guilty, visiting the iniquity of the fathers on the children and the children's children, to the third and fourth generation." How does Jonah chapter 3 show both God's mercy and the seriousness of sin?

* * * *

Now read aloud the article "A Repentant People," taking turns at the paragraph breaks.

A REPENTANT PEOPLE

5 minutes

The Ninevites' repentance is the most amazing event recorded in the book of Jonah, far more bizarre than the great fish or the rapidly growing plant. Through Jonah's terse, judgment-only message (frankly, the kind of thing we would be embarrassed to see written on a billboard as God's message to our neighbors), the Lord chose to save the people of Nineveh.

Remember, the Assyrians were notorious in the ancient world for their violence and disregard for life. Yet this people, out of all of the peoples in antiquity, uniquely believed the message from God's prophet and repented of their sins. Everyone from small to great became involved. They dressed in sackcloth and ashes as a sign of sorrow, and fasted as a sign of how deeply affected they were by their sin. They were so caught up they even involved their livestock in the outward signs of repentance.

They couldn't go on with life as if nothing had happened. They wouldn't simply confess their sin secretly and move on; they acknowledged publicly the gravity of their wrongdoing. Nor was their repentance limited to external rituals. The king commanded all of them to turn from their evil ways and forsake the violence that was in their hands and to call out mightily to God. Then who knows? Maybe, just maybe, there might be a future for them.

Did any prophet in Israel ever receive such a response as Jonah got from the Ninevites? Not one. Prophet after prophet spoke tenderly about the Lord's compassion for his people. They pleaded with the Israelites to turn from evil and return to the Lord. But though they knew the Lord by name, God's own people never responded with an outpouring of repentance like this. Even when the last and greatest prophet of all, Jesus of Nazareth, came to his own people with words of grace and truth, they rejected him. No wonder Jesus said the men of Nineveh would condemn those who heard his preaching. The Ninevites repented at the preaching of Jonah, and in Jesus Christ someone far greater had come!

This challenges each of us to ask if we have repented and responded to God's grace and mercy. Are we so different from ancient Israel? We have heard a far richer story of the Lord's love and grace to us in Jesus Christ. God offers us a much clearer message of salvation than he did the Ninevites, through a messenger who did not merely enter the margins of our world for one day but came and lived in our midst for more than thirty years.

Jesus is no Jonah: he came willingly, joyfully even, embracing the suffering that went with his calling, for the joy of redeeming a people for himself through his death and resurrection. This was necessary because God is gracious and merciful, yet also one who does not leave the guilty unpunished. Our guilt didn't just evaporate into nowhere; someone had to pay the price of our sin. At the cross, God took our sin seriously and judged it profoundly while still saving sinners graciously through simple faith in Christ.

As a result, Paul tells the Romans, "If you confess with your mouth that Jesus is Lord and believe in your heart that God raised him from the dead, you will be saved" (Romans 10:9). Repentance and faith in Christ surely lead to salvation and eternal life. Jesus's death washes away your sins, and his perfect righteousness clothes you and enables you to approach with boldness God's holy throne.

So how have you responded to this incredible good news? It's not enough to be a part of a Christian family or attend a Christian church. Jesus calls each of us to repent (turn from) our sinful determination to live life on our own. You don't have to don sackcloth and ashes. But you do need to acknowledge your sin, bow your knee to Christ, and recognize him as Lord of your life and your only hope of salvation. How will you escape death if you ignore such a wonderful salvation? The Ninevites will judge you too on the last day if you reject a far more gracious message than the one to which they so quickly responded.

And turning to God and away from our self-centered desires is not a one-and-done deal. We need to turn to God every day in repentance. Perhaps you need to repent of self-confidence in your correct theology. Correct theology is vital, but it is no substitute for Christ. It should lead us to deep humility instead of puffing us up with pride. Or perhaps you need to repent of your coldness toward outsiders that leaves you unwilling to share the gospel. Maybe you need to repent of your sense that you don't really need God's grace anymore, which makes you judgmental of believers who struggle. Or maybe you have become proud that you do know grace, which helps you identify all those Pharisees around you.

Yes, as Christians we need to repent. If this sounds troubling to you, understand that because of Jesus we do not repent out of fear. Rather than worry God is going to destroy us for our sins, we repent because our sins have been paid for in Christ. His death atones for us and his righteousness covers us. This means we are free to own up to the wrong that still indwells us. We dare to confess it all, confident in God's unchanging care for us. So come with joy, and bow your heart to him!

DISCUSSION *10 minutes*

When you realize you have to repent, how do you tend to feel about it? Do you think those feelings are normal for people? Are they the right feelings to have in that situation?

Like the people of Jesus's day who heard him preach in person, you know much more about Jesus than the people of Nineveh did. What do you know about Jesus that gives you good reasons to repent of sin?

Lesson

EXERCICE

REPENTANCE ROADBLOCKS

15 minutes

True repentance is a heart-level change that involves your whole person—what you believe, how you feel, and what you desire. We all tend to dislike this repentance and resist it. Whether you need to repent for the first time or are a Christian engaged in a lifetime of repentance, roadblocks might keep your heart from truly repenting. Read through the list of repentance roadblocks, noting some that seem to best describe you.*

REPENTANCE ROADBLOCKS

☐ **Putting off repentance.** Sin feels good at the moment, and repentance sounds like it will destroy you or suck all the fun from your life, so you avoid repenting for now.

☐ **Glossing over sin.** You imagine your sin only involves a few external missteps, or springs out of nowhere, so you match a shallow view of your sin with shallow repentance.

---

* The material in this exercise is derived in part from Serge discipling resources and from chapters 7 and 10 of Thomas Watson's book, *The Doctrine of Repentance* (Edinburgh: Banner of Truth, 1987). First published in 1668.

☐ **Fear and hiding.** Since repentance means admitting to God and others that you're sinful and broken, fear of exposure has you running *from* God when you need to be running *to* him.

☐ **Failure to pray.** You don't trust God's work in your heart to bring you to repentance (see 2 Timothy 2:25), so you seldom pray for a broken heart that hates sin, nor ask God to change you.

☐ **Failure to look at Jesus.** You forget that Christ covers your guilt and is renewing your heart, and you start to think everything depends on how well you change yourself. By looking at your own record instead of at Jesus, you lose your joy and gratitude, and you lose hope.

☐ **Failure to really fight.** You don't see how much honor there is in fighting alongside your Savior in his great battle against sin, so your "struggle" is really more like a habitual surrender.

☐ **Relying on willpower.** You resolve to start good habits or end bad ones, but you trust your own willpower instead of seeking God's power—forgetting that *you* are why you need to repent in the first place.

☐ **Cleaning up the mess instead of repenting.** You punish yourself or try to make up for what you've done, and you use this as a distraction to avoid actually repenting in your heart and finding forgiveness at the cross.

☐ **Talking about it instead of repenting.** You become an expert at the language and theology of repentance, so you say all the right things instead of actually repenting.

☐ **Regretting instead of repenting.** You're only sorry for what happened because of your sin, and not also sorrowful over how your heart loves sin.

☐ **Self-condemnation.** You avoid looking deeply at your sin because you can't handle the sad truth of what you'd see—and since you don't look deeply, you never repent deeply.

☐ **Thinking you're done because you quit a bad habit.** An external change that seems successful lulls you into thinking you don't need to repent anymore, or more fully.

☐ **Thinking it ought to be easy.** When you don't succeed immediately, and you realize you have a lifetime of repentance ahead of you that will require constant nearness to God, you decide it just doesn't work.

☐ **Other.** _____ .

Many of those repentance roadblocks come from not fully embracing who you are: both deeply sinful and deeply loved in Christ. In the same way, many of the most powerful motivations that can help you repent flow from the good news of Jesus. God's kindness is meant to lead you to repentance (Romans 2:4), so read through the list of gospel motivations and note some that might be helpful to you.

GOSPEL MOTIVATIONS FOR REPENTANCE

☐ **Your guilt is washed away.** In Christ, your sin is forgiven and you can own up to it—all of it—without any fear of condemnation.

☐ **You are clothed in the righteousness of Christ.** You are invited by God himself to come before his throne of grace and receive the help you need to fight sin (Hebrews 4:16).

☐ **Your shame is lifted.** The shame of your sin is far surpassed by the honor and dignity of being a child of God and a repentant person, one who drags sin out into the open where it can be killed.

☐ **You experience joy and love with your Father.** A repentant heart makes for great prayers that delight God and lets you enjoy your Father's forgiveness anew every day.

☐ **Repentance leads to celebration.** Times of repentance are the highlight of your life's story; they bring rejoicing in heaven (Luke 15:7).

☐ **God surely forgives you.** Repentance brings inward peace and a clear conscience, because God casts all your sins into the deepest part of the sea, utterly out of sight (Micah 7:19).

☐ **God surely helps you grow.** You can repent with confidence that the effort is worth it, because God promises to be at work in you to make you holy.

☐ **God has a glorious future for you.** Repentance is a taste of your coming life without sin and with God, which so captures your hopes that you long to start living that way now.

☐ **The cross shows the ugliness of your sin.** Realizing the cost Jesus paid for your sin helps you ignore sin's allure and see it for the filth it is.

☐ **Repentance is gratitude.** It flows from a thankful heart that has tears of joy for everything Jesus has done for you.

☐ **Repentance is how you love.** It is the best and sweetest love of all, because it is how you show love for God.

☐ **Repentance is a better life.** Seriously. Compare what you get with sin with what you get with God.

☐ **Repentance is the doorway to greatness.** A broken heart filled with sorrow for sin fits you for every godly task, making you compassionate, teachable, and ready to obey God.

Share some of your results with your group. How have you resisted repenting, and which motivations most encourage you?

WRAP-UP AND PRAYER

Because repentance is a grace received from God, one of the most important things you can do is pray regularly that God would work repentance in you. Begin praying now that he would teach you about your heart, give you brokenness over your sin, and make you hungry for a closer life with him.

8

THE GOD WHO RELENTS

BIG IDEA

God is not moody like you, and his mercies to you never fail or change.

BIBLE CONVERSATION *20 minutes*

After Jonah preaches in Nineveh and the people repent, a key change takes place in the story (though it is, as you shall see, in a sense no change at all). Have someone **read Jonah 3:5–4:2 aloud**. Then discuss the questions below.

When God relents from his plan to send disaster on Nineveh, do you find that surprising? Explain why or why not. If you do find it surprising, what about it is most surprising?

Compare God and Jonah in this passage. What stands out about the ways they are different?

Since the Ninevites were brutal enemies of God's people in Israel, it might seem obvious that the best way to care for his people would be for God to destroy Nineveh. But why might allowing Nineveh to survive (and eventually conquer Israel) actually be a better way for God to care for his people?

* * * *

Now read aloud the article "The God Who Does Not Change," taking turns at the paragraph breaks.

ARTICLE

THE GOD WHO DOES NOT CHANGE

5 minutes

For humans, repentance is generally a good thing, as it was for the Ninevites. We are so often headed in the wrong direction that it is refreshing for us to turn around and direct our steps back toward the way we should go. But does God ever repent? Does the eternal Creator change his mind and direct his steps differently, as this passage might suggest when it says God relented of the disaster he said he would bring on Nineveh?

No, the Bible says elsewhere that God does not change his mind, even pointing out in Malachi 3:6 how good this is because it's why Israel has not been destroyed for their persistent sin. Think about it: If God is perfect and always does what is right, then of course he never changes. I think the reason the Bible seems to speak of him changing his mind in Jonah is that God is accommodating himself to our way of looking at things—using baby talk.

Unlike us, the Lord dwells outside of time. He is never blindsided by unexpected events, never waiting nervously to see what we will do. Our actions don't shape him; his actions shape us, because he is the unchanging God who has determined the course of history from beginning to end. The Lord knew the Ninevites would cry out and he would deliver them, because he had planned that outcome before the foundation of the world. Indeed, he relents from judging the Ninevites precisely because he is consistent and faithful to himself. Throughout the Scriptures he is always a forgiving and merciful God. He always extends mercy to people who genuinely repent.

This makes God quite different from us. We are constantly surprised by people and circumstances. Someone cuts in front of you in traffic, and your anger flares. Then you get a call from your boss praising your presentation at work, and you completely forget your former anger. I experienced something like this recently. The evening before the flowers were due to arrive for my daughter's wedding, I clicked on the shipping status and saw to my horror the shipment was canceled by the supplier. We spent a sleepless night, but the next morning there was a new message that said, "Order at local distribution center." Our feelings changed rapidly!

Sometimes our angry responses reveal an idolatry. This week I became deeply frustrated when a trip to return some items to an office supply store was wasted because I didn't have with me the credit card used to buy them. Why was I so annoyed? In the family in which I grew up, waste was a cardinal sin, so wasting time because of my incompetence felt like an accusation of worthlessness. Our hearts swing from anger to joy and back again in a moment, driven by whether or not idols such as praise from the boss or good use of time are appeased.

But God is not like us in this, and that is where it gets challenging for Jonah and for us. Jonah wanted God to change and serve his agenda. Jonah thought the best thing would be for the Ninevites to be wiped off the map, which is not a crazy thought when you consider that over the next century they would become Israel's most brutal enemies. Jonah actually had the nerve to quote the Bible back at God, complaining that the Lord was a gracious and compassionate God who is slow to anger and abounding in steadfast love, as revealed in Exodus.

Jonah's problem was not really with the Ninevites. It was with the sovereign, gracious, unchanging character of God, who forgives wicked sinners and sanctifies his people through difficult circumstances. This is our fundamental problem as well, isn't it? We are angry with God because he won't change for us. He forgives people we think are undeserving, while insisting on taking us through traumatic trials that cause pain and heartache. Even our anger over trivial matters, like the traffic that makes us late or a forgotten credit card, is really anger at the God who rules those things. Like Jonah, we need to repent of our stubborn insistence that we should judge and govern the world.

Jonah missed out on celebrating the Father's joy over the repenting Ninevites because he was so committed to his own idea of justice. What about you and me? How much joy do we miss out on because we insist the Lord should conform to our agenda—which means making difficult people and situations go away, preferably in fiery flames? If you are like me, you have a resentful heart that holds grudges, and that resentment eats away at your joy.

That is why Jesus Christ came into this world. In Christ, the Lord's message for us is not *forty days and you will be destroyed*. Though we deserve such a fate, he pursues our resentful hearts and angry spirits and says to us, "How little you really know me! How much I love you, broken as you are, even though you hate to acknowledge it!" Jesus could have made all his enemies disappear in fiery judgment with a single word, but instead he modeled for us what it looks like to love our enemies and pray for those who persecute us—as he did when his enemies nailed him to the cross.

At that cross God was consistent, unchanging in being both the God who punishes wickedness and the God who forgives it. We can be sure all evil will one day be judged—either in Christ's death in our place, or in those who reject him. This enables us to trust God to take care of judging evil and frees us from feeling we need to make the guilty pay. And when we trust in Christ we can also be sure, even when we repeatedly fail to master our angry and resentful hearts, that his grace is sufficient for us. How much I still need to hear that truth!

DISCUSSION *10 minutes*

How does your experience with the way people constantly change moods spill over into your view of God? In his dealings with you, do you imagine God gets moody? Frustrated? Wondering if he'll have to resort to Plan B for your life?

If you constantly realized God is in control of the things that upset you and has a plan to use them for your good, how might it change your interactions with people who anger you?

Lesson

EXERCISE

REPENT OF TRYING TO GOVERN THE WORLD

15 minutes

Much of our sinful anger is like Jonah's. It comes from frustration that we can't get God to change the way he has decided to govern the world. As with any true repentance, repenting of our desire to be in charge involves examining our hearts and engaging God.

Use the chart to consider what this repentance might look like in your life. All the steps listed won't necessarily apply to everyone or happen in this exact order, but they generally reflect the way we can repent of trying to govern the world.

Recognize that you want to govern the world.
Deep in your heart, you think you know how the world should operate for everything to be right, and you find it frustrating when God doesn't order things that way. There are people you think ought to be judged and circumstances that should be resolved, yet God seemingly doesn't agree.

An example of how I want to govern the world is:

Confess that you are angry with God.
Admit to God that you are angry and resentful toward him. Your anger toward others actually reflects the fact that you continue to resist the Lord's sovereignty—even in those moments when your hands, feet, and voice are externally doing exactly what he says to do.

A resentment I need to confess to God is:

Delight in God's forgiveness.
God knows you through and through, and he will forgive you when you repent, as he always does. If you find it hard to repent, acknowledge that too, and ask for his help. Remember how God went out of his way to pursue unrepentant, self-righteous Jonah. So even if you too are slow to change, rejoice that God's forgiveness never changes.

One part of God's kindness that gives me joy is:

Own up to your struggle.
Find someone wise to share your struggles with, who will pray for you and encourage you while you struggle.

A way I might get support while I struggle is:

Celebrate the God who does not change.
As you experience the Lord's unchanging mercy in spite of your unrelentingly hard heart, you will show more of that same mercy to a lost world. And when you fail, as you often will, you will learn to run back quickly to the Lord from whom all repentance flows, knowing there is still mercy for you at the throne of his unchanging grace.

One thing I already love about the God who does not change is:

One way I can stay even more focused on God is:

Begin to love your neighbors.
Pondering God's grace will give you a startling joy in your weakness that enables you to love both friends and archenemies. Ask the Holy Spirit to help you behave better than you feel, loving those around you well, even when you are deeply angry with them.

An example of a way to love others even when I get angry is:

Share some of your findings with the group. How do you hope God will work in your heart?

WRAP-UP AND PRAYER *5 minutes*

If you are not yet a Christian, the unchanging nature of God is both good news and bad news. It means if you do not repent, you too must face his judgment. It may come in forty days or forty years, but the final outcome is sure: you will be weighed and found wanting against his standard of perfect justice. But the good news is if you bow before Christ, asking him to be your Savior, submitting your heart to his wise rule, then he will forgive all your sin and evil—every scrap of it—and clothe you in Christ's perfection instead. You can know this for sure because God does not change.

And Christian, this same gospel gives you the courage to face the continuing judgmentalism and thinking you are better than others that is in your heart without being overwhelmed by shame. Yes, you really are that bad, just as bad as all the people you are inclined to think are so much worse. But the grace of God is large enough to encompass your angry heart, and to enable you to start to love the lost people around you.

As you pray today, do so with confidence that the unchanging God will surely do his good work in you if you truly bow before him.

Lesson

9

IS IT GOOD THAT YOU ARE ANGRY?

BIG IDEA

Anger makes it hard for you to have compassion, and God would have you consider whether you are right to be angry.

BIBLE CONVERSATION *20 minutes*

The next lesson, also on Jonah 4, will focus on how God cared for Jonah by giving and then taking away the plant. But in today's lesson, you will spend more time looking at Jonah's anger. Have someone **read Jonah 4 aloud**. Then discuss the questions below.

Five simple words from Jonah had turned a notorious pagan city upside down in repentance. Most preachers would give their right arm for that kind of response. If Jonah had a godly attitude, what might you expect him to do next once he saw the Ninevites repented and God was not destroying them?

Jonah's actual response was to get angry and wish to die. What do you think made him so angry and despairing? (Think about not just the events happening in his life but also the attitudes of his heart.)

When God asked, "Do you do well to be angry?" the question should have sounded familiar to Jonah. Early in the Bible, the Lord asked Cain, "Why are you angry? . . . If you do well, will you not be accepted?" just before Cain murdered his brother Abel (Genesis 4:6–7). Based on what you know about anger, what are some reasons *Why are you angry* is a good question to ask?

*****

Now read the article "The Heart of Our Anger" aloud, taking turns at the paragraph breaks.

THE HEART OF OUR ANGER

5 minutes

In the 1970s, tennis player John McEnroe was famous for his on-court tantrums. One disputed line call would be enough to send him into orbit, shouting at the umpire. Have you ever felt like that toward God? Have you wanted to shout in his face, "You cannot be serious!" before tossing your racket and storming off the court of life? Of course you have—and so have I. Some of us may not show our anger quite so intensely; we coldly withdraw into ourselves and retreat from God and from those around us, refusing to pray or to engage. Yet whatever outward form our anger takes, the same heart attitudes Jonah exhibits in this chapter lurk within us all.

God asked Jonah if it was good for him to be angry. Paul Tripp has pointed out what a great counseling question this is.˙ The Lord didn't just tell Jonah to stop being angry or to stuff his emotions away. He invited him to bring out his emotions and examine them. Yes, you are angry, Jonah, but ask yourself, "Why am I angry? What is going on in my heart? What am I thinking about God, about myself, and about the world?"

---

* Paul David Tripp, "Disappointment with the God of Grace," a sermon on Jonah 4:1–4, October 21, 2007 at Tenth Presbyterian Church, Philadelphia, 22:25 timestamp. https://www.paultripp.com/sermons#!/swx/pp/media_archives/170495/episode/39323.

Whenever you find rage growing in your heart—whether it is with the car that cuts you off, or the child or spouse you are about ready to murder, or the roommate or coworker who is driving you nuts—ask yourself, is my anger good? Had Jonah examined his heart at this point, he might have recognized that his anger flowed from disappointed expectations about the Lord. How could God let those Assyrians off scot-free?

It is true that there is such a thing as good anger. Jesus was rightly angry over the evil he saw around him—for example, false teachers. But much of our anger is not in line with God's thinking. Anger blinds us to the truth and twists our thoughts even about the Bible, as it did with Jonah when he quoted Scripture while angry, so we should be very suspicious of our anger. We should assume that even when we bring our anger out into the open and examine it, we often won't be able to sort out our feelings without wise people to help us. And even when the root cause of our anger is righteous, our expression of it will be mixed.

Our anger often flows from disappointment with God's purposes. Why do I get angry at my spouse's sins and shortcomings? It is because I believe the Lord owes me a perfect spouse, or at least a nearly perfect one, not the sinner I actually married. The Lord has the power to sanctify my children instantly but for some reason he refrains from doing so, which makes home life a complicated affair.

And then there is me. I'm angry with God over the fact that my same sins, which have hurt those around me so deeply, keep triumphing over me. Lord, even though you tell me to run into your presence just as I am, that would be too painful because I would have to confess my sin and repent of it. So why don't I just run away and sulk for a while? My coldness toward God and lack of an intimate prayer life is just another form of anger, entirely natural for someone like me who has never screamed at an umpire in his life.

Like Cain, Jonah didn't answer the Lord's question. Instead he went out in silence and sat down to see what would happen. Maybe the Lord would sort out his wrong view of mercy, and judge the Ninevites after all. If Jonah had the power to slay the Ninevites himself, he surely would have done so. But since he lacked that power, his anger turned inward and he asked for his own death instead. Just kill me now, God, rather than make me endure one more day in a universe that doesn't live by my rules.

Of course, the irony is that if the Lord had been like Jonah, quick to kill those who didn't deserve forgiveness, Jonah would have died long before this. He received grace upon grace, but he failed to show that same grace to others. When the Lord came back with the same counseling question he had asked earlier—are you right to be angry now over a plant?—Jonah exploded with self-justification: "Yes, I do well to be angry, angry enough to die." Jonah was so convinced of his own rightness that it seems nothing in all creation could change his mind.

Grace should have changed Jonah. Even more, it should change us. We know Jesus, who lived out the perfect righteousness we need. Jesus didn't run from the Father's command; he delighted in it. He didn't sit to the east of Jerusalem, calling down fire from heaven to destroy the place that would crucify him. Instead, he wept over it and called down the Father's forgiveness. Now his righteous commitment to view the world through his Father's eyes is credited to you in place of your angry heart. His perfect love and compassion clothes you and makes you perfectly acceptable to God.

This love should convince us to trust God's wisdom. When you explore your anger and ask if it is good, examine it in the light of the cross. The grace upon grace we have received should move us to great compassion for others. Are they desperately wicked sinners? So too are we. Do they deserve our forgiveness? Neither did we deserve God's forgiveness. As we meditate on this love and mercy, it will still the storm in our heart and invite us to emerge from our self-made shelter in the burning wilderness. We will find rest in our true home and refuge, Jesus himself.

DISCUSSION *10 minutes*

Imagine you are hunkering down with Jonah to the east of your personal Nineveh. What are you watching in anger, hoping it gets destroyed? (In picking something to share, watch out that you don't gossip about others.)

Now you answer the question Jonah ignored: Is it good for you to be angry? What is going on in your heart?

EXERCISE

INTERROGATE YOUR FEELINGS

15 minutes

Rather than deny or embrace your feelings, the Bible offers a third approach: interrogate your feelings. Question your anger and be honest about its sinful and selfish elements, and about what the gospel says to you when you get angry.

To start interrogating your feelings, read through this list of feelings and behaviors Jonah had, noting those that sound familiar in your own life.

EXPLOSIVENESS

Jonah: Lashed out in tirades when things didn't go his way. Quick to get angry about how God is slow to anger.

Me: Full of yelling and hurtful words, or specializing in criticism and complaints. Quick to get angry and find fault, whether in a loud tone or one that remains calm.

SULKING

Jonah: Went off by himself to pout.

Me: Tend to retreat from others to let my unhappiness simmer, refusing to interact with those who make me angry or challenge my motives. May snap, "I'm FINE!"—by which I really mean Frustrated, Insecure, Neurotic, and Exhausted.

DESPAIR

Jonah: Was so angry he wished to die.

Me: Not able to see any way my situation ends well. Ready to give up on God being good to me.

GRUDGE-HOLDING

Jonah: Refused to let his dislike for Nineveh change even after the people repented.

Me: Keep holding against people how they have hurt me in the past. Unable to get beyond their sinful tendencies that annoy me.

LACK OF COMPASSION FOR THE LOST

Jonah: Gave no pause even to the thought of children and animals being destroyed in Nineveh.

Me: Unconcerned over coworkers, neighbors, family who don't yet know Christ as their Savior because I'm preoccupied with my own concerns and agendas.

RESENTMENT

Jonah: Couldn't stand to see the Ninevites get off so easily.

Me: Can't stand to see life go well for others—as when they have recognition, happiness, or romantic relationships I don't, or when they "get off lightly" for their sin.

COLDNESS TOWARD OTHERS' SPIRITUAL PROGRESS

Jonah: Did not rejoice at the Ninevites' repentance nor stick around to teach them further. May have scoffed at their sackcloth and ashes, or that ridiculous display of dressing up their animals.

Me: Full of "discernment," able to pick apart the spiritual lives of others and be critical about progress that gives them joy. Could find a way to be grouchy, and pronounce that God is displeased about something, even in the midst of the world's greatest spiritual revival.

BIBLE MISUSE

Jonah: Expressed disgust at the truth about God from the book of Exodus, citing it to legitimize his anger.

Me: Good at avoiding the Bible when I'm angry with God and don't want my sin confronted, and a master at quoting it selectively to get a self-serving application.

SELF-FOCUS

Jonah: Quick to notice how everything affected him, repeatedly using I, me, and my in his prayer in verses 2 and 3.

Me: Usually think my evaluation of what is right must be correct, and my concerns are God's concerns. Often sure my church is better, my way of parenting is better, my political views are better, et cetera—and others could learn from me.

Now consider what the gospel has to say about your anger. Pick a few truths that might be particularly helpful to you, based on how you need to repent. Then share some of your results with the group.

☐ I am a sinner too, and God has given me mercy so many times in so many ways! "From his fullness we have all received, grace upon grace" (John 1:16).

☐ I can look back in my life and see times when, like Jonah, I deserved judgment. Of all the people who have gotten off lightly for their sin, I am the prime example. "Christ Jesus came into the world to save sinners, of whom I am the foremost" (1 Timothy 1:15).

☐ God is patient with me, gently training me even though I am slow to learn. "Your right hand supported me, and your gentleness made me great" (Psalm 18:35).

☐ God will not let evil go unpunished forever. I can leave it in his hands to dole out just the right justice and mercy. "Do not say, 'I will repay evil'; wait for the LORD, and he will deliver you (Proverbs 20:22).

☐ God has planned everything in my life—even the frustrating things—for my good. "For those who love God all things work together for good" (Romans 8:28).

☐ My reputation does not depend on me being right, respected, or treated well. Those things are dead to me compared to the greater honor of being in Christ. "For you have died, and your life is hidden with Christ in God. When Christ who is your life appears, then you also will appear with him in glory" (Colossians 3:3–4).

☐ My Father loves me. He invites me to leave all my frustrations with him. "Casting all your anxieties on him, because he cares for you" (1 Peter 5:7).

☐ To know that Jesus died for *me* is all the me I need. "It is no longer I who live, but Christ who lives in me. And the life I now live in the flesh I live by faith in the Son of God, who loved me and gave himself for me" (Galatians 2:20).

☐ Jesus is angry at evil but still full of compassion for sinners—
and God's work is to make me more like him! "And we all,
with unveiled face, beholding the glory of the Lord, are being
transformed into the same image from one degree of glory to
another" (2 Corinthians 3:18).

WRAP-UP AND PRAYER

Spend your remaining time together in prayer. Be sure to include
prayers that God would grant you true repentance, from the heart.

Lesson

10

MERCIES AND TRIALS

BIG IDEA

God uses both mercies and trials in your life to pursue your heart with great compassion, and to save you from evils around you and the evil within.

BIBLE CONVERSATION *20 minutes*

Your study of Jonah ends with this lesson. Start by having someone **read all of Jonah 4 aloud**. Then discuss the questions.

The book of Jonah would have finished on a high note if it had ended with chapter 3, so why does chapter 4 exist at all? What do we learn about God merely from the fact that he wants us to know this part of the story?

What are several ways you might describe God's pursuit of Jonah? Think in terms of what God did, how he did it, and why he did it.

God used both mercy (the plant) and a trial (the scorching wind) to get Jonah's attention. How does having both mercies and trials in one's life encourage a person to draw nearer to God?

* * * *

Now read aloud the article "Deliver Us from Evil," taking turns at the paragraph breaks.

DELIVER US FROM EVIL

5 minutes

Back in chapter one of Jonah, the Lord demonstrated his power to calm a storm on the sea when it threatened to engulf Jonah and the sailors. Here at the end of the book, we find ourselves asking whether the Lord can calm the storm that is raging inside Jonah as well. And can he also quiet similar storms when they rage in our hearts?

God's response to Jonah's anger continues to be grace. Some people worry that sooner or later, with all their sin, they will finally anger God enough that he'll say, "That's it! I've had it with you!" But instead of giving Jonah the judgment he deserved, the Lord once again intervened to rescue him, this time with shelter from the hot sun. *Evil* is a theme word in the book of Jonah, and in Hebrew it can mean both moral evil and trouble or disaster. Literally, the text says the purpose of the plant was to save Jonah from his evil.

We are told Jonah was exceedingly happy—as happy about the plant as he had earlier been angry about the Ninevites. That statement is very revealing of Jonah's heart. Jonah spends almost the entire book being bummed out as the Lord shows him grace upon grace. However, the one thing that makes him smile is a little divine air conditioning. He would be quite content to see an entire city roast in hell, but he was overjoyed over a plant whose only purpose was to make his personal life a little easier.

It would almost be funny if it weren't quite so close to home. What makes you exceedingly glad? Whatever it is exposes your primary values. I rejoice about all kinds of little things, like seeing my name mentioned on a blog or being praised by my friends. If your chief idol is fame, you will be exceedingly glad for praise. If it is money, you will be exceedingly glad when your bank account grows. And so on. Joy can be a diagnostic tool to help you see your idols more clearly, just as anger can.

But the Lord brings trials as well as joys. Sometimes we get squeamish about God's sovereignty over trials. We might say God *allowed* the cancer or he *permitted* the accident because we want to distance God from active responsibility for painful things. But the book of Jonah won't let us divide the world so easily. The Lord appointed the plant to shade Jonah, and then he appointed the worm that killed the plant and a wind that roasted the prophet. There is no distinction here.

Jonah's suffering is a sign of God's uncomfortable grace. If the Lord had wanted to punish Jonah, there are far hotter places he could have sent him. Instead, he wanted to hold up a mirror to Jonah. "Do you really want justice, Jonah? Do you really want fire from heaven to descend on those who disobey the Lord? You can't even handle a hot wind! Do you really want to store up hot anger in your heart?" The Lord was challenging Jonah's prideful anger to invite him into deeper fellowship where he could acknowledge his need of grace and see the Lord's amazing patience with him.

I'd love to tell you that Jonah was convicted of his sin and ready to pray the Lord's Prayer—*deliver me from evil.* Yet his heart seemed so hard at this point that neither God's kindness nor his sternness would reach it. Jonah had asked over and over for death, and you or I might have been tempted to give the prophet what he was begging for, but the Lord didn't. Strikingly and fittingly, the Lord gets the final words in the book, and those are words of mercy and compassion.

It may seem odd to describe Jonah's attitude toward the plant as compassion (or pity), but it highlights the contrast between him and the Lord. Jonah cared about the plant and wanted it spared, even though he had done nothing to bring it into existence or sustain it. His feelings for the plant were shallow self-interest. But the Lord *did* work to create this world and all it contains, humans and animals alike. He sustains them every day. Doesn't that give him the right to show compassion and spare some of them, evil though they are? And won't this be a deep compassion, flowing out of love rather than self-interest?

We don't know how Jonah responded to the Lord's final words, because what matters is not how Jonah responded but how you and I respond today. In a sense, Jonah was absolutely right that the Ninevites deserved to die for their sins. So did Jonah. So do you and I. But we have seen the ultimate act of the Father's compassion in the person of Jesus Christ.

In the garden of Gethsemane, Jesus echoed the Greek translation of Jonah 4:9. Where Jonah was "sorrowful unto death" over the plant, Jesus's soul was "sorrowful, even to death" over the suffering of the cross (Matthew 26:38). But whereas Jonah was ready to die rather than surrender his belief that the Ninevites should be damned, Jesus was ready to die rather than surrender his commitment that his people should be saved. Jonah was ready to die out of anger, Jesus was ready to die out of compassion.

Jesus went outside the city that rejected him and submitted to the Father's burning wrath, of which the scorching east wind was a pale parody. He hung on a cross without shelter or shade, so that he himself might become our shelter from the judgment of God. As we meditate upon the Lord's consistent grace to us, it will enable us to acknowledge the sin within us. And we will begin to turn from it, to the God who delivers us from all evil.

DISCUSSION *10 minutes*

Think about the two kinds of evil in your life—troubles and sin. Which more often makes you turn to God for deliverance? Why is that?

The article suggests the Lord was inviting Jonah into deeper fellowship so Jonah could learn his need for grace and see the Lord's patience. What about you? What might God be inviting you to learn and see as he invites you into deeper fellowship with him?

Lesson

EXERCISE

JOYS AND TRIALS (REVISITED)

15 minutes

Now that you've been through the book of Jonah, let's see how your thoughts about the joys and trials of your life may have changed. This is the same exercise you had in lesson 1. Consider once again how you might complete these sentences about the joys and trials of your life, and be ready to discuss your responses.

JOYS

Something in my life that has made me very happy is

_____ .

A little thing in my life that always gives me joy is

_____ .

One thing I've learned about myself, by considering what makes me happy, is

_____ .

One thing God has taught me about himself, through his grace in my life, is

_____ .

TRIALS

A particularly difficult trial in my life was/is

_____ .

A little thing that always irks me or makes me sad is

_____ .

One thing I've learned about myself, by considering my trials and what makes me angry or sad, is

_____ .

One thing God has taught me about himself, through the trials in my life, is

_____ .

Now share some of your findings with the group. If you notice any pattern in how God deals with you, tell about that.

WRAP-UP AND PRAYER *5 minutes*

As part of your prayer time, you might want to thank God for what he has taught you in Jonah and ask him to keep teaching you from his Word.

LEADER'S NOTES

These notes provide additional thoughts from the author and from the editor who composed the study questions. In some cases, they provide further background the group may find helpful. In other cases, they give direction for leading the study or hints as to some good ways to answer the questions. The discussion leader should read these notes before the study begins.

Occasionally, the discussion leader may want to refer the group to a point found in the notes (for example, if a particular question about the text comes up, or if the group seems hopelessly lost on a certain question). But it is important that you not treat these notes as a way to look up the "right answer." In most cases, the best answers will be those the group discovers on its own through reading and thinking about the Bible passages and articles. In fact, you will be disappointed if you turn here expecting answers to each question. In most cases these are general notes, not question-by-question answers.

LESSON 1: NOT JUST A FISH STORY

BACKGROUND NOTE: IS JONAH HISTORICAL? Some participants may wonder about the historicity of the events described in Jonah. Sincere Christians disagree about whether or not the surprising stories actually happened. Some suggest the unusual events are intentional indicators on the part of the author that this story is a parable, not an account of history. But other prophetic narratives contain plenty of surprising events as well, such as Elijah being fed by ravens in the wilderness (1 Kings 17:6) or the donkey that speaks to Balaam (Numbers 2:28–30). And, of course, anyone who confesses the most surprising reality of all—that the infinite God became incarnate in a little baby and then died on a cross for our sins—should have little difficulty with anything else surprising that God does in the Bible. To me, the most compelling evidences for this being a true historical story are twofold: First, it ascribes a historical name to the central character, Jonah ben Amittai, a prophet whose name is recorded in Israel's history in 2 Kings 14:25. It is one thing to tell a parable about an imagined individual, but ascribing fictional events and attitudes to a real person is quite different. Second, Jesus himself appears to have regarded the events of this story as involving real, historical people. He said that just as Jonah was three days and nights in the belly of the fish, so too the Son of Man would be three days and nights in the heart of the earth. What's more, Jesus added that the men of Nineveh will rise up on the day of judgment and condemn the generation that rejected him (Matthew 12:38–42). For these reasons, I think it is best to understand this as an account of real—though certainly surprising—events that do not merely *tell* us something about God that would have to be validated in some other way, but rather *show* us something real and true about God.*

BIBLE CONVERSATION

The book of Jonah is about the Lord's unlikely compassion on broken people, and the self-righteous prophet's stubborn determination to resist it. The center of the story, however, is not the ugliness of Jonah's heart—though that is laid bare for all to see; it is the Lord's gracious and unrelenting pursuit of him in spite of his self-righteousness. Ironically enough, the main message of the book is found on the lips of the reluctant prophet himself, when he declares, "Salvation belongs to the Lord!" (2:9). That is, the Lord decides whom he will deliver from their evil and whom he will pass by. Everyone in the story needs mercy; there is none who can stand on his own merits. And if salvation belongs to the Lord, then no one else gets to decide who does and who does not qualify for the Lord's mercy. That is precisely the lesson that Jonah himself is so slow to learn.

---

* For a fuller defense of the historicity of Jonah, see R. Reed Lessing, *Jonah*, Concordia Commentary (St. Louis: Concordia, 2007), 3–13.

ARTICLE DISCUSSION

These discussion questions are the first of many that will ask participants to share how they feel about God, whether good or bad. Keep the tone honest and inviting, and not pushy. Some people may not be ready to share right away during the first lesson. It helps if the leader is willing to share honestly, especially about struggles with sin.

EXERCISE

In this exercise and in many of the others, some participants may feel stuck because they cannot come up with a response for every single part of it. Encourage them simply to respond where they can and not worry about the rest. The point of the exercises is not to complete an assignment, but to get participants thinking and talking about life with God.

LESSON 2: RUNNING FROM GOD

BIBLE CONVERSATION

The text doesn't tell us explicitly in this chapter what Jonah's motives for running were. Some have suggested he was afraid of the Assyrians. One commentator compares sending an Israelite to preach to Nineveh in the eighth century BC with sending a Jew to preach to Berlin in the 1930s.** Yet Jonah does not appear to be someone who would easily be overawed by such a challenge. He had already brought the Lord's Word faithfully to an unfaithful king of Israel. He didn't seem frightened in the least by the terrible storm on the sea, either. So, it seems fear was not his primary motive for flight. In fact, Jonah himself tells us his motive in chapter 4. If the Assyrians continued to exist, and their repentance proved short-lived, then they might in the future be an even bigger threat to Israel.

** Phillip Cary, *Jonah*, Brazos Theological Commentary on the Bible (Grand Rapids, MI: Brazos, 2008), 40.

Jonah didn't just flee from Nineveh, he fled from the Lord's own presence. He turned in his badge and gun, as it were, resigning his commission as a prophet because of his irreconcilable differences with his employer. Nor did he just quit his job; he also quit actively practicing his faith. Theoretically, he may still have believed he feared the Lord, as he told the sailors. But compare Jonah's attitude to that of the psalmist in Psalm 27, for whom the one thing he desired was to dwell in the Lord's house forever, gazing on his beauty. As a prophet of the Lord, Jonah had the privilege of standing in the Lord's very presence, yet he fled from there and from the Lord's land, trying to get as far away from the Lord as he could. Even though his words were still theologically orthodox, Jonah had functionally given up on his faith in the Lord. Of course, there is an inconsistency in Jonah's thinking here. He didn't quit when God told him to go and preach a message of grace to Jeroboam II, even though Jeroboam was an evil king who would persist in his wickedness. That was different, in Jonah's eyes. He figured the Lord was allowed to show such grace to his own people, even when they didn't deserve it. But for Jonah, showing the same grace to outsiders like the Assyrians was a step too far.

Face-to-face with the reality of the Lord's judgment, Jonah preferred to continue to hide from God. Even when the ship's captain woke him and told him to cry out to his god, he still did nothing. Although it was part of a prophet's job to intercede for people, the last thing Jonah wanted to do was bring himself to the Lord's attention. He was determined to continue his flight from God, even if it meant perishing in the storm. Forced to identify himself, Jonah did confess that he feared (or worshiped) the Lord of heaven who made the sea and land. But there was little evidence that Jonah actually did fear the Lord at that moment: he was a picture of calmness in contrast to the pagan sailors who were appropriately terrified when they heard he was fleeing from the presence of God.

Jonah's answer when the sailors asked what to do with him is also revealing. It should have been evident at this point that Jonah's flight from the Lord was not going to be successful. Yet there is no hint of any attempt on Jonah's part to repent of his sin and ask for the Lord's forgiveness, much less any attempt to seek a new opportunity to obey. Jonah had no desire to receive grace and mercy from the Lord; he would rather be judged by strict justice. In contrast, the pagan sailors who had cried out to many different gods ended up fearing the Lord, even offering a sacrifice and making vows. They were utterly transformed by their encounter with Jonah's God. Jonah was less affected.

ARTICLE DISCUSSION

When God does things we don't think he should do, or when he doesn't do the things we think he should, we are tempted to flee from him. Our expectations of God are high, which is not necessarily bad if they are based on God's wonderful promises in his Word to bless us and to change us, making us better and holier people. Yet our experience of life is often low, as we face many challenges and difficulties. Life is hard and so is lasting change. Our circumstances are not what we hoped and neither are we. We typically respond to this discrepancy between our hopes and our experiences in one of two ways: we either pretend our experience matches our hopes, thus living in denial about the difficulties and pain of life, or we bring down our expectations to match our reality and give up expecting God to answer our prayers. The better way is to trust God and come near to him, even when he contradicts our desires and will. Only then are we really fearing the Lord.

EXERCISE

For some participants, this exercise might focus on struggles with sin and how we sometimes draw back from God when our progress in holy living seems slow. Once again, our basic problem is that we are not willing to accept the reality of the God we claim to serve—one who is sovereign over sanctification as well as the other parts of salvation. We are happy with him as long as he is working on our agenda to fix the things we want to have fixed, but very frustrated when our timeline seems to slip and we feel we are going backward rather than forward. We resist the truth the pagan sailors recognized, that the Lord does as he pleases (1:14).

LESSON 3: REDEEMING THE RUNAWAYS

BIBLE CONVERSATION

Most of the ways Jesus is different from his disciples and Jonah stem from how he is quick to trust God the Father and completely willing to obey him. So, it is not surprising that he would mention faith when the disciples were scared. A person of faith relies on God, believing God's promises are true and his commands are good. Well-placed faith in God would make the disciples much more like Jesus. Faith in God enables us to be calm in times of trouble and also to obey God in times of temptation. Jesus believed this when he agreed to die on the cross. He fully trusted the Father to care for him, body and soul, quoting Psalm 31 with his dying breath: "Father, into your hands I commit my spirit!" (Luke 23:46).

ARTICLE DISCUSSION

Among other things, hard times in our lives might help us find comfort in God alone rather than in worldly joys, and they might drive us to come closer to God in prayer, Bible reading, Christian fellowship, et cetera. Our inability to prevent our own suffering teaches us humility and trains us to rely on God's power alone. It assures us that God is our loving Father, and his correction is a sign of how much he loves us as his children. It helps us to rely on him so we endure difficult things and place our hope in the life to come rather than in the fleeting joys of this world. Hard times and sinful failings also give us compassion for others who struggle, and our sufferings give us a kinship with Christ who also suffered in his time on earth.

The fact that Jesus also suffered assures us, first of all, that if we believe in him any hard times we experience are not a punishment from God or an expression of his anger. Jesus took our punishment and made us God's children so our suffering has become part of his fatherly care and ultimately serves to bring us nearer to him. Secondly, even Jesus was made perfect through suffering (Hebrews 2:10) and learned obedience that way (Hebrews 5:8), so we can be encouraged that our suffering too is making us into people fit to glorify God forever, with great joy. The fact that Jesus was tempted in every way we are means temptations are a normal part of the Christian life, ordained by God (see Matthew 4:1) as a way for us to grow in grace. It means Jesus is able to sympathize with us in our weaknesses, encouraging us to come near to him to receive help and mercy when we too are tempted (Hebrews 4:14–16). And it assures us that in every way we fail, Christ has succeeded on our behalf so every sin is paid for and we stand fully righteous before God.

EXERCISE

(Leader: You may want to read this aloud to your group after doing the exercise.)

One point of this exercise is to show that determined self-effort (the scrambling sailor) is hardly different from little effort (the sleeping Jonah) at its core. In both, we turn inward and are self-absorbed instead of turning to God. Both are forms of pride: either we think we are able to solve our own problems, or we think our problems are so deep and so special that God is unable or unwilling to intervene for us.

One constant danger as we learn to live by faith rather than self-effort is that what we call faith might actually become another form of self-reliance. For example, good habits of faith that are meant to turn our focus to Christ—such as prayer, Bible reading, and church attendance—can become ways we instead keep the focus on ourselves; rather than feeling encouraged about Jesus, we instead feel encouraged or discouraged about ourselves based on how well we stick to those habits. So, be careful not to let your discussion of faith turn it into just another way you need to row harder. Faith is received from God, not created out of your own strength. And it is about who you trust, not how well you trust.

LESSON 4: SALVATION IS OF THE LORD

BIBLE CONVERSATION

As the waters closed over Jonah, he went down into the heart of the seas, down to the very base of the mountains, down to the entry gate of Sheol itself, where he felt the bars of the underworld closing in upon him. It seemed there was no possible way back into the Lord's presence for him; he had been driven out of the Lord's sight, and life and light were gone forever. But as Psalm 139 makes clear, even the realm of the dead is not able to keep out the presence of the living God. Like the prodigal son in the far country, it was in that most hopeless of circumstances that Jonah's heart started to change. As his life ebbed away and he felt utterly and deservedly abandoned by God, he prayed. Distant though he was from the Lord's presence in the temple, spiritually as well as physically, his prayer nonetheless came to the Lord there, and the Lord lifted him up from the pit (Jonah 2:6–7).

It is interesting that Jonah prays his acknowledgment psalm while he is still in the belly of the fish, before he has been returned to dry land. Normally you wouldn't write that type of psalm until after you'd been rescued. Yet even while physically still inside the fish, Jonah feels rescued. He was remarkably confident that the Lord would indeed show him mercy and return him to the land of the living, where he could once again journey to the temple and offer sacrifices with God's people.

Many people read this psalm as evidence of a total transformation on the part of Jonah. We are told he has come to see the error of his ways, and now recognizes the Lord alone is sovereign over salvation. However, I'm not sure Jonah has been so completely transformed yet. He is clear about the sovereignty of God in his situation, and that is good. He notes that it was the Lord who cast him into the heart of the seas, not just the sailors. The waves and billows that passed over him were the Lord's waves and billows (v. 3), and it was the Lord who delivered him from the pit (v. 6). Yet there is no true repentance here. In sending him down to the very gates of Sheol, the Lord simply turned Jonah over to himself and gave him what he was pursuing. There is none of the language of the penitential psalms, and no attempt on Jonah's part to take responsibility for his own actions in the way David does in Psalm 51. Jonah is grateful the Lord has rescued him from his difficulties, but he doesn't seem able to recognize his own fault in all of this.

The specific word used to describe how Jonah was vomited out of the fish may be a clue to understanding Jonah's attitude. It's an unusual word that is primarily used to describe physical vomiting because you have eaten or drunk too much, but significantly it is also the word used in Leviticus 18:25 to describe the promised land expelling its inhabitants into exile because of their abominable sin.

What this means is the message of this chapter is not that we should repent as Jonah does and learn to be like him; it is that we should repent as Jonah doesn't. Jonah may have been redeemed and delivered from death, but he hasn't yet been deeply changed by his experience of grace. Like the unmerciful servant in the parable Jesus told, he is joyful because all his debts have been forgiven and he has been set free, but he doesn't yet grasp the enormity of that debt and therefore lacks love and compassion toward other sinners. He thinks of them as merely idol worshipers who don't deserve anything from the Lord, unlike upstanding prophets like him who deserve God's grace when they mess up. And yet, remarkably enough, in spite of his self-righteousness and confusion, the Lord still delivers him from the pit and will recommission him to go a second time as his prophet. How great indeed is God's grace!

ARTICLE DISCUSSION

Rationalizing away your sin is one mark of the extent to which you view yourself as a natural insider to grace. "I didn't do that," I exclaim. "Or even if I did, it really wasn't what you thought. There is some perfectly justifiable reason for my actions, and if you weren't so thickheaded it would be obvious to you." I utter lots of self-justifying prayers for help, especially when I am at the end of my rope like Jonah and experiencing the painful death my sin brings into my life. I expect God to help me, because after all, I am part of his people. So God really owes it to me. If we start thinking this way, it might be helpful to remember Jonah's deliverance was not automatic—it was sheer grace. Disobedient prophets don't always live to tell the tale in the Bible. After the unnamed prophet in 1 Kings 13 was tricked into disobeying the Lord's very specific instructions for his mission, he met a lion on the way home and had a much less edifying encounter with nature than Jonah. There is no necessary reason why the fish should be there to rescue Jonah rather than be a fitting final resting place for the prophet, a cautionary tale of warning for others.

A main point of this lesson is God is actively involved in his people's lives. Whether you tend to think he is sitting back being pleased with you or sitting there disgusted, the truth is he is not sitting back at all. He is actively with you, sovereignly in control of his good plan to work in your heart and bring you safely home.

EXERCISE

As an example of the kind of insight this exercise might draw out, consider how seminary professors like me might be prone to theological pride (found under the KNOWING THE TRUTH heading). We have advanced theological degrees in removing the speck from others' eyes, while all the time missing the log in our own eyes. We know exactly how much of each garden herb should be tithed, while missing justice and mercy (see Matthew 23:23). Yet if God really is sovereign, as our theology rightly proclaims, then he is sovereign over other people's defective theology, as well as over the differences in their culture, over their lesser academic background, and over their other weaknesses. Maybe there are things other Christians bring to the body of Christ that we don't, such as a passionate love for the lost, perhaps, or a biblical concern about creating a more just society.

LESSON 5:
FULL JUDGMENT, FULL SALVATION

BIBLE CONVERSATION

Jesus points out two ways he is like Jonah. First, there is the one sign: just as Jonah essentially died and came back to life through his encounter with the fish, Jesus too endured a judgment-of-God death and emerged alive. Second, Jonah's success with a foreign city that repented is another foreshadowing of Jesus. Jesus too preached in gentile territory (see Matthew 15:21–28), and after his resurrection he sent out his disciples to extend the preaching of repentance and mercy to all nations (see Luke 24:46–47). So when Jesus cites Jonah, he seems to be aware that in descending to earth his mission is to die as a judgment for sin and come back to life so anyone in the world who believes may be saved. See, for example, how he described his mission when he spoke to Nicodemus in John 3:13–18.

ARTICLE DISCUSSION

One goal of this lesson is to make sure as we look inward and examine our hearts we also look outward to Jesus, in whom we are saved and find our hearts changing. Try to keep that encouragement front and center.

EXERCISE

See Romans 6:1–11 for a discussion of the truth that believers are united with Christ in both his death and resurrection.

LESSON 6:
THE MOST DIFFICULT AREAS OF LIFE

BIBLE CONVERSATION

When Jonah sinfully ran away from his calling, the Lord did not simply write him off and condemn him to the fate he deserved. God graciously offered Jonah another opportunity to do what he was told to do in the first place. This is an important aspect of the teaching of the book of Jonah: our God is a gracious and merciful God who deals with us far more patiently than we deserve. He is not, as we are sometimes tempted to imagine, a harsh parent just waiting for us to mess up so he can tell us once again how useless we are and kick us out of the house. God is a loving parent who cares far too much for Jonah to leave him in rebellion. The Lord continues to come after Jonah. The prophet cannot escape the difficult task of going to Nineveh, nor the requirement that he wrestle with the coldness in his own heart. This means the Lord's second call to Jonah is a test as much as it is an opportunity.

Jonah is still a reluctant prophet. The three days it took to travel across Nineveh makes Jonah's visit there strangely reminiscent of his time in the belly of the fish, but it seems Jonah wasn't any more eager to spend time in his new location than he was in the fish. He doesn't tell the Ninevites anything about the Lord, as he did with the sailors, or even mention the Lord's name. Grace might enable the Ninevites to avoid the coming judgment, but Jonah doesn't say a word about his own recent experience of deliverance, which he had spoken of so eloquently while still inside the fish. After all of the Lord's graciousness to Jonah in delivering him from the very gates of Sheol and giving him another opportunity, there doesn't seem to be much real change in Jonah's heart.

Instead, he simply says, "Forty days, and Nineveh shall be overthrown!" There is no "Come now, let us reason together, says the LORD: though your sins are like scarlet, they shall be as white as snow," as the prophet Isaiah said (Isaiah 1:18).

If Jonah had been confronted over his message, he doubtless would have responded by saying he had done what the Lord commanded him. But the way in which he did it reveals the hardness of his heart, and it is often the same for us. Our lack of love for others is exposed in the carelessness with which we fulfill our mandate from the Lord to bring them the good news of salvation in Christ in the first place and the ongoing good news of the Lord's grace to them as justified sinners. We either don't bother to share the gospel with them at all, or if we do, we are motivated primarily by pride or guilt so we leave satisfied if we have "done our duty" and spoken the truth—uncaring about whether we have presented it in the best possible way to communicate the Lord's undying love for sinful people. We may be quite good at pronouncing judgment on one another, but not nearly as good at speaking grace. Do you take the evidence of God's grace in your life and apply that same generous gospel to those who wrong you and hurt you?

We might also note that Jonah appears to go to Nineveh in his own will-power, as if he intends to show God that this time he will obey, rather than relying on the Lord's strength. The closeness to God that seemed present when Jonah was crying out from inside the fish is now missing. Jonah seeks God's help in times of distress, but there's no evidence he does the same when it comes to serving or obeying God.

ARTICLE DISCUSSION

This discussion is an example of a time when the leader should be prepared to share about his or her own struggles, which might help participants be willing to share about theirs.

EXERCISE

Note that the rest of Hebrews 12, which builds on Proverbs 3:11–12, goes into more detail about how the training in righteousness we receive from our Father gives us confidence when we struggle to remain faithful to him, and reverence and awe when we worship him.

LESSON 7: A CALL TO REPENT

BACKGROUND NOTE: DID THE NINEVITES TRULY REPENT? One question that may come up is whether the Ninevites' repentance was real. Were they really part of God's eternally chosen people, or were they simply trying to save their own lives from the fiery judgment to come? I'm not sure we can completely answer that question, but I think at least some of them must have been genuinely repentant, or Jesus's assertion in Matthew 12:41 that the men of Nineveh would condemn the people of his own day for their unbelief would have no force. It may not have changed their society for any significant length of time—by a few years later, the Assyrians would be embarking once again on brutal campaigns of world domination. But at least for some of them, for a brief period, I believe there was real heart repentance and change in response to Jonah's preaching.

BIBLE CONVERSATION

Only God could bring about such an immediate, positive response to Jonah's deeply flawed presentation of the truth. The Ninevites didn't need to be swallowed by a big fish or even to face an enormous storm to turn them around. They simply believed God. And like Abraham in Genesis 15:6, "he counted it to him as righteousness." They didn't know much about this God in whom they were believing. That is why the narrator carefully uses the generic word God for the one in whom they believed rather than the Lord's personal name, which is used with the sacrifices and vows of the pagan sailors in chapter 1. The Ninevites also didn't know whether God would pay any attention to their repentance or would destroy them anyway. Yet from the greatest to the least, they repented to such an extent that it was impossible not to notice the results.

Putting sackcloth on the livestock may seem like a crazy thing to do. After all, sheep and cattle can't sin, so how could they repent? Yet there was a certain logic to this action: if Nineveh were to be destroyed, the animals would share the same fate as its inhabitants. And even though the image of domestic animals in sackcloth outfits is undoubtedly comic, the effect certainly conveys the deadly seriousness of the Ninevites.

The repentance of the Ninevites, and God's forgiveness that followed, is a preview of the era following Christ's resurrection when "repentance and forgiveness of sins should be proclaimed in his name to all nations" (Luke 24:47). It was always God's plan to extend repentance to the whole world. In fact, there are other hints that foreigners would be quickest to repent. The Lord told the prophet Ezekiel if he had sent him to foreigners they would have responded to his message readily, but as it was, he would find the Lord's people a hard and closed audience (see Ezekiel 3:4–7).

ARTICLE DISCUSSION

There is no single, right answer to the question about feelings. It's common for repentance to feel like death. After all, we are crucifying our sin! But there is also a lasting joy that comes from growing closer to God, a joy that comes when we have an authentic repentance accompanied by believing the gospel.

EXERCISE

The discussion leader should be alert for several unhelpful tendencies that could pop up in the discussion of repentance. The first is groveling. It is important we learn to see ourselves through God's eyes, which means we are not only *deeply sinful* but also deeply loved. If the deeply sinful side of this starts to turn into self-bashing, remind participants that repentance is an honorable act that is central to who we are as dearly loved children of God.

Secondly, it's easy to start thinking repentance is something we need to conjure up from some goodness of our own. Rather than believe this, we need to understand that repentance is *received* from God by his work in our hearts. This means running around trying to fix our outward behavior is not our main role in the process. Instead, we must focus on preparing to receive his grace: we confess our sin to God, we pray he will break our hearts and help us hate that sin, and we learn to love Jesus by feeding on his Word privately and with others.

Finally, we must never let our dependence on God become an excuse to delay repentance or keep sinning. Sin is always dangerous to the soul. It would be a grave mistake to think we may continue in a particular sin while waiting for the Spirit to make us feel more repentant in the heart. Repentance is always incomplete in this lifetime, but the time to stop sinning is now. We should quit our sinful acts, and set up accountability or make amends if needed, even if our heart hasn't yet reached the point of a fully biblical repentance.

LESSON 8: THE GOD WHO RELENTS

BACKGROUND NOTE: What Christians call *repentance* means deciding that your former behavior has been wrong and declaring that you will seek to move in a different direction in the future. This is a central idea in both the Old and New Testaments. In Greek, the word used for repenting is *metanoeo*, which literally means "to change your mind," while the most common Hebrew verb for this concept is *shub*, which is often translated "to turn." Another Hebrew verb that conveys similar ideas is *nacham*, which is often translated "to relent" or "to regret." Both of these Hebrew words are used in our passage in chapter

3:9, in the question the king of Nineveh asked about the unknown God who had threatened judgment on his city.

The question of whether or not God changes his mind also comes up in 1 Samuel 15:29. There we are told that, unlike human beings, God does not lie or change his mind (*nacham*). Some people would suggest there's a contradiction between that passage and ours in Jonah. But actually, the tension is already there within the passage in 1 Samuel 15. There we are also told twice that God does *nacham* when it comes to having appointed Saul as king over Israel (verses 11 and 35). Also, later in 2 Samuel 24:16 there is an exact parallel to the usage in Jonah: the Lord *nachams* of the catastrophe he had planned to bring upon the city of Jerusalem and does not do it. So it is not that one biblical writer is contradicting another. It is rather that there is one sense in which God can be said to *nacham*—to change his mind, to relent, to regret something he did earlier—and another sense in which it is insulting even to think that of God. As suggested in this lesson's article, I think God is accommodating himself to our perspective and speaking in terms of the way things appear from our vantage point when he speaks of changing. Yet God dwells outside of time and not only knows the end from the beginning but is sovereign over everything that happens in between so his actions are never reactions to unforeseen and unexpected events. From an eternal perspective, there is no change in God.

BIBLE CONVERSATION

The Lord's mercy on Nineveh should not be much of a surprise given what has already taken place in the book of Jonah. In the first chapter, the sailors were threatened by a terrible storm from the Lord, but when they threw Jonah overboard, the storm grew still and they were safe. In the second chapter, Jonah was driven out of the Lord's presence because of his sin, yet when he cried out the Lord sent a great fish to deliver him. Here, having threatened the Ninevites with total destruction, the Lord relented when they repented.

This unchanging mercy of God is present throughout Scripture. Ironically, when the king of Nineveh said, "God may turn and relent," he was unconsciously quoting Joel 2:13. This means Israelite readers ought not to have been surprised. They had seen the Lord behave that way to them, over and over again. The unexpected aspect of the story is not that God relents when people repent; it is that he does so for Gentiles rather than just for his chosen people. Remarkably enough, God was pursuing a relationship with these wicked Ninevites, inviting them to interact with him personally and discover his unchanging goodness and grace. It is always our repentance that is surprising rather than God's response to that repentance.

Also note that there is actually a subtle ambiguity in the phrasing of Jonah's message to Nineveh that hints this is what the Lord had in mind all along. Literally, what Jonah 3:4 says is not, "Forty days, and Nineveh shall be overthrown" but, "Forty days, and Nineveh will be overturned." It's a fine distinction, and one Jonah himself probably missed. After all, this verb is used often in the Old Testament to describe destruction, as in the case of Sodom and Gomorrah (Genesis 19:25), which is exactly what Jonah was hoping to see happen to Nineveh. Yet the same verb is also used in Esther 9 to refer to the turning upside down of the fortunes of the Jews. On the very day when they were supposed to be annihilated, the Lord gave them a stunning victory over their enemies. It thus leaves open the question of whether the impending overturning is one of destruction or salvation, a move from life to death or from death to life.

You should realize that the repentance of the Ninevites was short-lived. The positive change we see here was replaced equally quickly by a negative change that took them back to their old ways. Over the next century, the Assyrians would be brutal perpetrators of horrific war crimes. They would make the Israelites' worst nightmares come true, culminating in the death of many people and their exile from their land. Life would have been much easier for the Israelites without the ongoing threat of the Assyrians.

Yet the Lord's purpose was not to give Israel an easy life; it was to sanctify them. He was going to deal with their sin, and if they had only been willing to repent as the Ninevites did, their story could have turned out so much differently. But in the Lord's sovereignty, he combined his plan to judge his unrepentant people for their ongoing wickedness with his plan for the good news to go to the Gentiles and touch their hearts, even if only briefly, to demonstrate that salvation truly is of the Lord alone.

ARTICLE DISCUSSION

Even if our correct theology means we know very well that God does not get moody or frustrated, on an emotional level we are still inclined to react as if he does. So, it is important that we let the truth of who God is—he is unchanging!—guide our feelings about him.

EXERCISE

Although this exercise is arranged as a chart that helps participants see some clear steps they can take to repentance, it's important not to treat it as a formula. Remember that repentance is received from God, and we don't control him. We can't make his work in our hearts happen a certain way, or on our schedule, by following a formula. However, we *are* called to stop our sin and to participate in our own repentance by depending on God and preparing our hearts for his work, which is the focus of this exercise.

LESSON 9: IS IT GOOD THAT YOU ARE ANGRY?

BIBLE CONVERSATION

Jonah was the prophet whose words had the most immediate and profound impact on his audience in recorded history. Yet Jonah's response was not to join the Ninevites in their rejoicing and to instruct them more fully in the way of redemption. Instead, he had a heart malady: he was angry with God. He had a self-focused attitude that crystallized into a determined conviction that his perspective alone made sense out of the universe. He alone was fit to be the true judge of what was right in the world. Often, we blame our life situation—relationship, family, or job troubles—for our anger. But our circumstances are merely the soil in which the seeds of anger and depression grow. They expose a heart malady that lies dormant during the easy times. In fact, for Jonah it was not failure but success that made him angry with God. And he was every bit as angry as Cain had been back in Genesis—angry enough to see someone end up dead.

It is easy to judge Jonah and marvel at his hard-heartedness, but how often do we behave in the same way toward God? Whenever we sin, we are in that moment living out of our evaluation of what is important in the world, while rejecting the Lord's evaluation. We are saying that we alone can determine what our true needs are, not God and the Scriptures. We need this pleasure and we need it now; God has no business refusing us what we want, and the whole world should revolve around our way of thinking. Because such attitudes are so often at the heart of our anger, and even mixed in when our anger is appropriate, it is good for us to consider why we are angry.

We might also consider what plan God has for us that he has allowed us to survive despite our anger. Jonah could have been drowned in the sea, digested by the fish, or stoned to death by an angry mob in Nineveh. And yet he survived by God's mercy and compassion alone, free to pray his angry prayers against the Lord, free to sulk and pout. How is our situation similar?

ARTICLE DISCUSSION

Encourage participants to open up about their struggles with anger. Talking about it will help them be aware of it and repent. But because other people are often the target of our anger, also be careful that this part of the lesson does not become an opportunity for gossip. The focus should be on the anger of the person sharing, not the sin of whomever they are angry with. And in some cases, to avoid gossip, some participants should not talk about some of their anger in a group setting.

EXERCISE

Try to help participants be specific in giving examples of how they are like Jonah: "What happens when you get resentful? What does it look like to others when you sulk?" For example, Jonah used Bible verses (Exodus 34:6–7 about God's compassion and Joel 2:13 about how God relents from bringing trouble) to legitimize his rebellion against God. And just as Satan twisted God's word in the garden, we too can use it to support all manner of evil. A specific example might be that we use the biblical principle of male headship to browbeat our wives into submission, or we might use the biblical command to be gentle and compassionate with one another as an excuse to avoid ever having to confront sin. Perhaps we argue that because Jesus says his kingdom is not of this world, we don't have to be involved in seeking to transform our community, or because the Lord is sovereign in evangelism, we really don't have to take the trouble to pursue our neighbors with the gospel.

LESSON 10: MERCIES AND TRIALS

BIBLE CONVERSATION

If the story of Jonah had ended with the conversion of the Ninevites, we would have learned much about God's concern for the lost but not so much about his pursuit of individuals like you and me, who need God to work on our hearts. At the time God first called him to go to Nineveh, Jonah may not have even realized there was a problem with his heart. He probably thought he was willing to do whatever God asked of him. If there had been a Jerusalem missions conference, he might have been among the first with his hand up to volunteer. It was only when the call became specific that he discovered the ugly truth about his heart. And it was only after the Lord relented from destroying Nineveh that Jonah learned the full depth of that ugliness. That's why the story of Jonah doesn't end with the conversion of the Ninevites but continues on into chapter 4, which shows us more of the Lord's interaction with Jonah, confronting his angry and bitter heart. Also notice that at the start of chapter 4 Jonah not only needs to repent; he also is bitterly unhappy. Jonah's joy is at stake here, and that's why in the final section of the book the Lord will lovingly continue to pursue Jonah out into the wilderness, probing his heart.

The Lord who can make a giant fish to swallow Jonah can just as easily bring forth a giant plant in exactly the right spot to shade Jonah from his distress, or a worm to kill the plant. After all, as Jonah himself confessed, the Lord is the God of the dry ground as well as of the sea (1:9). Notice the very ordinariness of the means the Lord uses at the end. The book of Jonah is full of enormous creatures and surprising events that clearly display the Lord's sovereignty. But the final act of the Lord's sovereignty in this story is so small and ordinary that it might pass by our attention altogether. What could be more ordinary than a little bug eating a plant? I've never seen a great storm dramatically silenced, an enormous fish swallow a person, or an entire city converted by one sermon. But I see worms consuming plants in my garden all the time. You see the point: the Lord is sovereign over the tiniest of details of life just as much as he is over the dramatic events. He is sovereign over the slowly leaking tire on your car just as much as he is over the terrible accident in which you should have died but you walk away without a scratch. He is sovereign over your bad night's sleep and your headache just as he is sovereign over the cancer diagnosis.

Notice too that the Lord is sovereign over the trials of life as well as over the joys of life. And once again we see the Lord's goal in this bitter providence was not to destroy Jonah but to pursue his heart: "Let me give you an environment that will match the heat in your heart."

ARTICLE DISCUSSION

Participants may like to know more about how *evil* is a theme word in the book of Jonah, the Hebrew word being the same for both moral evil and catastrophic disaster. Jonah was sent to prophesy to the Ninevites in the first place because their evil (sinful behavior) had come up before the Lord (1:2). The focus of the story then shifts from the evil of the Ninevites to the evil (trouble) of Jonah and the sailors. The crew of the ship cast lots to find out on whose account this evil (trouble) had come upon them (1:7). The answer was Jonah's evil (sinful behavior) in running away from the Lord (1:10). Yet the Lord had mercy on Jonah and forgave him, rescuing him from the grip of Sheol. The Lord, we may say, delivered him from his evil and restored his feet to solid ground. In the second half of the story, Jonah finally obeyed God's command and preached to Nineveh. As soon as Jonah declared the coming judgment, the Ninevites repented. The king urged everyone to turn from their evil ways (sinful behavior) and they did so (3:8). In return, God relented from the evil (trouble) he had said he would do to them (3:10). As he had done for Jonah, so too the Lord delivered the Ninevites from their evil.

EXERCISE

It may seem odd to critique our joys. But as the article pointed out, the things that give us joy reveal our top priorities, and these can be idols. Jesus delighted to do the Father's will. He told his disciples, "My food is to do the will of him who sent me and to accomplish his work" (John 4:34). Is that how you view life? Is that your primary joy? I am often ambivalent about the prospect of serving God. My first question is whether serving God will make me happy, bring me satisfaction, be enjoyable—because if it isn't, I may still do it, but don't expect me to like it.

mission
propelled by good news

At Serge we believe that mission begins through the gospel of Jesus Christ bringing God's grace into the lives of believers. This good news also sustains and empowers us to cross nations and cultures to bring the gospel of grace to those whom God is calling to himself.

As a cross-denominational, reformed sending agency with more than two hundred missionaries and twenty-five teams in five continents, we are always looking for people who are ready to take the next step in sharing Christ through:

- **Short-term Teams:** One- to two-week trips oriented around serving overseas ministries while equipping the local church for mission

- **Internships:** Eight-week to nine-month opportunities to learn about missions through serving with our overseas ministry teams

- **Apprenticeships:** Intensive twelve- to twenty-four month training and ministry opportunities for those discerning their call to cross-cultural ministry

- **Career:** One- to five-year appointments designed to nurture you for a lifetime of ministry

 Grace at the Fray   **Visit us online at: serge.org/mission**

www.newgrowthpress.com

spiritual renewal resources for you

Disciples who are motivated and empowered by grace to reach out to a broken world are handmade, not mass-produced. Serge intentionally grows disciples through curricula, discipleship experiences, and training programs.

Resources for Every Stage of Growth

Serge offers grace-based, gospel-centered studies for every stage of the Christian journey. Every level of our materials focuses on essential aspects of how the Spirit transforms and motivates us through the gospel of Jesus Christ.

- **101**: The Gospel-Centered Series
  Gospel-centered studies on Christian growth, community, work, parenting, and more.
- **201**: The Gospel Transformation Series
  These studies go a step deeper into gospel transformation, involve homework and more in-depth Bible study
- **301**: The Sonship Course and Serge Individual Mentoring

Mentored Sonship

For more than twenty-five years Serge has been discipling ministry leaders around the world through our Sonship course to help them experience the freedom and joy of having the gospel transform every part of their lives. A personal discipler will help you apply what you are learning to the daily struggles and situations you face, as well as, model what a gospel-centered faith looks and feels like.

Discipler Training Course

Serge's Discipler Training Course helps you gain biblical understanding and practical wisdom you need to disciple others so they experience substantive, lasting growth in their lives. Available for on-site training or via distance learning, our training programs are ideal for ministry leaders, small group leaders or those seeking to grow in their ability to disciple effectively.

 Grace at the Fray   **Find more resources at serge.org**

resources and mentoring
for every stage of
growth

Every day around the world, Serge teams help people develop and deepen a living, breathing, growing relationship with Jesus. We help people connect with God in ways that are genuinely grace-motivated and increase desire and ability to reach out to others. No matter where you are along the way, we have a series that is right for you.

101: The Gospel-Centered Series

Our *Gospel-Centered* series is simple, deep, and transformative. Each *Gospel-Centered* lesson features an easy-to-read article and provides challenging discussion questions and application questions. Best of all, no outside preparation on the part of the participants is needed! They are perfect for small groups, those who are seeking to develop "gospel DNA" in their organizations and leaders, and contexts where people are still wrestling with what it means to follow Jesus.

201: The Gospel Transformation Series

Our *Gospel Transformation* studies take the themes introduced in our 101-level materials and expand and deepen them. Designed for those seeking to grow through directly studying Scripture, each *Gospel Transformation* lesson helps participants grow in the way they understand and experience God's grace. Ideal for small groups, individuals who are ready for more, and one-on-one mentoring, *Gospel Identity, Gospel Growth,* and *Gospel Love* provide substantive material, in easy-to-use, manageable sized studies.

The Sonship Course and Individual Mentoring from Serge

Developed for use with our own missionaries and used for over twenty-five years with thousands of Christian leaders in every corner of the world, Sonship sets the standard for whole-person, life transformation through the gospel. Designed to be used with a mentor or in groups ready for a high investment with each other, each lesson focuses on the type of "inductive heart study" that brings about change from the inside out.

 Grace at the Fray

Visit us online at serge.org

www.newgrowthpress.com